Elaine Hunter is ... runs the Deperso... London and Maudsley NHS Foundation Trust. She started researching depersonalisation/derealisation disorder in 1999 and has published many of the key papers from a psychological perspective on the condition, including a cognitive behavioural model and a treatment trial.

Dawn Baker is a chartered psychologist and trained therapist in Cognitive Behavioural Therapy (CBT). She has worked at the Depersonalisation Research Unit at the Institute of Psychiatry, King's College London, developing a psychological model of depersonalisation disorder as well as treatment and management strategies. She is now retired.

Emma Lawrence is a Clinical Psychologist with a particular interest in mind-body interactions and is currently working in a physical health setting. Prior to this, she was a Lecturer at the Institute of Psychiatry, King's College London, conducting research on emotion processing and regulation to include work on depersonalisation. She also has an ongoing interest in mindfulness-based approaches.

Anthony David was appointed Consultant Psychiatrist at the South London and Maudsley NHS Foundation Trust and Senior Lecturer in Psychiatry at the Institute of Psychiatry in 1990. He was awarded personal chair of the Institute in 1996 and was, until recently, Chairman of the British Neuropsychiatry Association. In 1998 he set up the first clinic for depersonalisation disorder in the UK (the Depersonalisation Research Unit).

Contributing authors **Nick Medford** and **Mauricio Sierra** are both clinical psychiatrists working at the Depersonalisation Research Unit at the Institute of Psychiatry. Dr Sierra originally qualified in Colombia and undertook his PhD on depersonalisation at Cambridge University. Dr Medford worked in neurology before training in psychiatry at the South London and Maudsley NHS Foundation Trust.

The aim of the **Overcoming** series is to enable people with a range of common problems and disorders to take control of their own recovery programme.

Each title, with its specially tailored programme, is devised by a practising clinician using the latest techniques of cognitive behavioural therapy – techniques that have been shown to be highly effective in changing the way patients think about themselves and their problems.

Many books in the **Overcoming** series are recommended under the Reading Well scheme.

Other titles in the series include:

OVERCOMING ALCOHOL MISUSE, 2ND EDITION

OVERCOMING ANGER AND IRRITABILITY, 2ND EDITION

OVERCOMING ANOREXIA NERVOSA

OVERCOMING ANXIETY, 2ND EDITION

OVERCOMING BODY IMAGE PROBLEMS INCLUDING DYSMORPHIC DISORDER

OVERCOMING BULIMIA NERVOSA AND BINGE-EATING, 3RD EDITION

OVERCOMING CHILDHOOD TRAUMA

OVERCOMING CHRONIC FATIGUE

OVERCOMING CHRONIC PAIN

OVERCOMING GAMBLING ADDICTION, 2ND EDITION

OVERCOMING GRIEF

OVERCOMING HEALTH ANXIETY

OVERCOMING HOARDING

OVERCOMING INSOMNIA AND SLEEP PROBLEMS

OVERCOMING LOW SELF-ESTEEM, 2ND EDITION

OVERCOMING MILD TRAUMATIC BRAIN INJURY AND POST-CONCUSSION SYMPTOMS

OVERCOMING MOOD SWINGS

OVERCOMING OBSESSIVE COMPULSIVE DISORDER

OVERCOMING PANIC, 2ND EDITION

OVERCOMING PARANOID AND SUSPICIOUS THOUGHTS, 2ND EDITION

OVERCOMING PERFECTIONISM, 2ND EDITION

OVERCOMING RELATIONSHIP PROBLEMS, 2ND EDITION

OVERCOMING SEXUAL PROBLEMS, 2ND EDITION

OVERCOMING SOCIAL ANXIETY AND SHYNESS, 2ND EDITION

OVERCOMING STRESS

OVERCOMING TRAUMATIC STRESS, 2ND EDITION

OVERCOMING WEIGHT PROBLEMS

OVERCOMING WORRY AND GENERALISED ANXIETY DISORDER, 2ND EDITION

OVERCOMING YOUR CHILD'S FEARS AND WORRIES

OVERCOMING YOUR CHILD'S SHYNESS AND SOCIAL ANXIETY

STOP SMOKING NOW, 2ND EDITION

OVERCOMING DEPERSONALISATION AND FEELINGS OF UNREALITY

2nd Edition

A self-help guide using cognitive behavioural techniques

OVERCOMING

ELAINE HUNTER,
DAWN BAKER, EMMA LAWRENCE
and ANTHONY DAVID

ROBINSON

ROBINSON

First published in Great Britain in 2007 by Robinson, an imprint of
Constable & Robinson Ltd

This revised and updated edition published in 2018 by Robinson

3 5 7 9 10 8 6 4

Important Note
This book is not intended as a substitute for medical advice or treatment.
Any person with a condition requiring medical attention should consult a
qualified medical practitioner or suitable therapist.

ISBN: 978-1-47214-063-0

Typeset in Bembo by Initial Typesetting Services, Edinburgh

Printed and bound by CPI Group (UK) Ltd, Croydon, CR0 4YY

Papers used by Robinson are from well-managed forests and other
responsible sources

Robinson
An imprint of
Little, Brown Book Group
Carmelite House
50 Victoria Embankment
London EC4Y 0DZ
An Hachette UK Company
www.hachette.co.uk

www.littlebrown.co.uk

Contents

PART ONE:
Understanding DPAFU

PART TWO:
Overcoming DPAFU

Acknowledgements

The Depersonalisation Research Unit at the Institute of Psychiatry, Psychology and Neuroscience, London, opened in 1998 and was the first unit in the UK to specialise in depersonalisation and feelings of unreality (DPAFU). The unit was in part set up by a grant from the Pilkington family charities, to whom we are hugely indebted. The Pilkington family have shown enduring faith in our work and have continued to encourage us to improve our understanding of the condition and, hopefully, help to overcome it.

The launch of the unit was marked by an article in *The Times* by Dr Thomas Stuttaford (12 March 1998), which prompted a flood of enquiries from people seeking more information and help. The unit was initially co-directed by psychiatrist Mary Phillips, whose work on emotion and the brain helped increase our appreciation of DPAFU and what might cause it. Many other individuals have contributed to the clinic over the years as psychologists and psychiatrists, including Carl Senior PhD, Poppy Schoenberg PhD, Dr Michele Lambert, Dr Maxine Patel and numerous visitors from abroad. In addition, work in the US by Dr Daphne Simeon's group and in Germany by Dr Matthias Michal's group has added to our knowledge about this condition and has therefore been drawn on throughout the book. The research undertaken in our unit has also been supported by various additional funding agencies such as the Medical Research Council and the Wellcome Trust.

Most importantly, however, we would like to thank the people who experience DPAFU and who have agreed to take part in the numerous research studies our unit has conducted. The research unit continues today and has expanded to include a specialist clinical service within the South London and Maudsley National Health Service Foundation Trust, which offers assessment and treatment to adults with depersonalisation/derealisation disorder. Referrals must come through a general practitioner, mental health professional or psychiatrist.

We also have some very personal acknowledgements we wish to make:

Elaine
To my son, Hercules Phillips.

Dawn
For what the universe has given me.

Emma
With gratitude to my teachers.

Anthony
For Philip and Gloria Pilkington.

Preface

This book has been produced by a team of clinicians and academics who have worked for the Depersonalisation Research Unit at the Institute of Psychiatry, Psychology and Neuroscience and the Depersonalisation Disorder Service clinic, King's College, London. The unit conducts various research projects and the clinic offers assessment and treatment to people who experience depersonalisation/ derealisation disorder and feelings of unreality (DPAFU).

The book will help you to understand and manage your DPAFU using highly effective Cognitive Behavioural Therapy (CBT) strategies. Numerous research studies have shown that CBT works extremely well with a variety of different types of people and problems. There may be a range of benefits derived from the techniques we suggest here. In some people with DPAFU, these strategies may help the problems all but disappear. With others, the severity of the problems may reduce to the extent that the person can get on with their life again. In other cases, the frequency or duration of the DPAFU may lessen. In working through this book, you are likely to feel more in control of your problems, better able to cope and better able to function in your day-to-day life. We can't promise this book will provide you with a complete cure since there may be factors beyond the scope of this book that need to be addressed, but you will learn strategies that are likely to have a positive impact on helping you feel better.

Using principles derived from CBT does not mean that physical and biochemical aspects of DPAFU are not important. We will discuss these physical and biochemical aspects, along with medical (i.e. drug) and other treatments for depersonalisation disorder. And although we believe the strategies we outline are likely to be of real benefit, this book isn't intended to be a replacement for treatment or therapy. If you feel you need to talk to a professional about your problems, then your GP may be able to help. If he or she can't help, a referral to a clinical psychologist, psychiatrist or CBT therapist may be appropriate.

The CBT approach helps people to look at the connections between how and what they *think*, how they *feel* and how they *behave*. The theory suggests that our personal life experiences, adversities and mood states can influence our thoughts, beliefs and values, causing them to become biased or distorted. This can mean that unhelpful thoughts and thinking patterns are likely to occur. These can lead to negative feelings such as loss of confidence or feeling low and anxious. In turn, when you feel low or anxious you often change your behaviour. For instance, you may feel less like socialising, and so you go out less. If you go out less, you may end up feeling lonely, which, in turn, leads to a lower mood. This can develop into a downward spiral that feels difficult to break on your own. This cycle will then lead to a continuation and potential exacerbation of the original problem. Only once the problem has been identified, and you are able to see why it is continuing, can you then think about how you would like things to be different. The changes you want to make can become your goals and you can become more focused in achieving these goals. This self-help guide will help you through that process.

The key ideas from CBT are:

- It is not what happens but how you *interpret* the experience that matters.
- How you think, or your appraisal about a situation or experience, will influence how you feel and behave.
- How you behave affects what you think and how you feel.
- Your emotional and physical state will influence your thoughts and behaviour.
- Our thoughts, emotions and behaviours are all connected and each influences the other.

The key components of CBT treatment are:

- To identify and define your core problem(s) and how they influence your everyday life.
- Once a problem is defined, you need to identify the things that you do (or don't do) that lead to the problem continuing. These could include:
  - Unhelpful behaviours – for example, taking drugs or avoiding situations
  - Unhelpful thinking patterns – such as focusing on the worst-case scenario
  - Negative emotional states – like hopelessness or numbness
  - Focusing on physical sensations – such as visual disturbances
- You need to set out clear and specific changes that you would like to make. These then become the goals to work towards during CBT.
- The idea is then actively to work on achieving these goals using the variety of techniques set out in this book.
- Throughout this process, you will be encouraged to evaluate your progress. This will involve recognising what is working well and not so well. You can then draw up new goals to help you use what you've learned and apply this knowledge to other situations.
- In essence, you will become your own therapist.

PART ONE

UNDERSTANDING DPAFU

1

What is DPAFU?

Depersonalisation is most simply defined by feelings of unreality and detachment. This can be about your sense of self, your emotions, thoughts, memories and physical sensations. Derealisation is a sense of unreality and detachment about the external world. Most people experience both depersonalisation and derealisation at the same time and so the problem is commonly called depersonalisation/derealisation disorder, although it is possible to have just one or the other. Alongside the key sensations of unreality and disconnection, there are a wide range of other symptoms that form part of the spectrum of symptoms. These include emotional and physical numbing as well as problems with thinking and perception. We will outline these more in this chapter.

One of the defining characteristics of depersonalisation and derealisation that makes it distinct from other mental health problems is profound *feelings of unreality* about everything and of being *disconnected or cut off from other people and the world*, often with a sense of there being a physical barrier between the person and the outside world. People generally find it extremely difficult to describe these experiences, and usually use metaphors such as being 'in a dream' or 'inside a bubble' or 'viewing the world from behind glass'. There can be a sense of being cut off from one's own sense of self, with doubts and confusion about one's own identity. For instance, some people describe how their reflection in the mirror, or the sound of their own voice, can seem unfamiliar to them.

With derealisation, the external world looks dream-like and unreal. This can mean that familiar places appear foreign (also known as '*jamais vu*') and that streets and build-ings look like 2D stage sets. Other people can also appear robotic or alien, too.

Another very common symptom of DPAFU is *emotional numbing,* to both positive and negative emotions. This may include a lack of empathy or affection, even towards those close to them. On an intellectual level, you may be able to say that, in circumstance 'A', you should feel happy and, in circumstance 'B', you should feel sad, but you may have difficulty experiencing these feelings. This can make people feel as if they are no longer human as their emotional responses feel numbed.

People with DPAFU can report that their *actions feel robotic*, as if they were on automatic pilot and 'spectators' of their own activities – like watching a movie or TV programme of their own lives. Their thoughts, speech and actions no longer feel spontaneous. However, even though people with DPAFU feel they are robotic and on automatic pilot, this is not noticeable or obvious to other people.

Many of those with DPAFU describe physical numbing, where all their body, or parts of it, may feel numb as if they have had an injection of local anaesthetic. Some people can't feel the weight of their body or don't feel they are inhabiting their body anymore. Others describe a sense of a physical change in a specific part of their body, such as their head feeling large or that their body feels like a hollow shell. People often report looking at their face or hands and, although intellectually they know these belong to them, they don't feel emotionally or physically connected to these parts of themselves. In some people, the sense of numbness or unreality about their body is so intense that they touch or pinch themselves repeatedly to try to feel 'normal' again.

Cognitive numbing with impaired thinking, concentrating, remembering and using visual imagery are also commonly reported. Sometimes people will use the phrase 'brain fog' to describe how difficult it is to process information as if one's head has been filled with cotton wool. These symptoms can cause problems with study or work, or even with everyday tasks such as reading.

In addition to the above symptoms, some people experience visual distortions. These include their vision seeming blurred or out of focus (even though their eyesight has tested normal), objects appearing 2D rather than 3D or larger or smaller, and colours losing their vibrancy. There can also be sensory distortions with sounds appearing muffled and food losing its taste.

One of the unusual aspects of DPAFU is that it is a completely subjective experience, in that these symptoms are not noticeable by other people, even when very severe. You may have noticed that the phrase 'as if' crops up a lot in these descriptions. This is very important because it shows that people don't really believe their head is full of cotton wool, or that they really are watching life go by on film. It's just a way of trying to capture their strange experience and describe it to someone else. From the psychiatrist's or psychologist's point of view, this is crucial. Saying 'as if' means that the experience is different from a delusion (a false belief) or a hallucination (when we perceive something that isn't there) and so requires a different approach and different treatment.

As well as the direct problems with DPAFU, lots of people affected with DPAFU also report significant levels of *anxiety*. This can take the form of panic attacks, repetitive intrusive and distressing thoughts, a fear of going out alone, intense anxiety in social situations, or a tendency to worry too much. Others may also experience low mood or depression. This is often a result of the impact of the DPAFU when they feel sad about how they are affected by it or hopeless about getting better.

Some people, however, are not visibly anxious or depressed but may be quite introverted or preoccupied. Those with DPAFU often talk of an intense state of absorption in which they focus intently on these feelings. This state of absorption may intensify the symptoms, leading to a vicious circle. They spend a lot of time dwelling on their thoughts and may appear wrapped up in their own world. It's quite common for them to spend excessive amounts of time worrying about abstract, existential or metaphysical issues, such as the meanings of words, how other people experience the world, the meaning of life and concepts of space and time.

How do I know if I have DPAFU?

Have a look at the checklist below that describes some of the main sensations associated with DPAFU. Put a tick next to each of the statements according to how often you experience these sensations in your everyday life.

Checklist of Main DPAFU Sensations

Main DPAFU sensations	Never	Sometimes	Often
Changes to feelings and emotions			
Feeling cut off or detached from the world around you			X
Being emotionally numb		X	
Lacking feelings towards other people, such as affection	X		
Feeling in a dream-like state			X
Feeling like a robot or on 'automatic pilot'			X
Loss of motivation due to everything seeming without meaning		X	
Feeling isolated from the world around you			X

Main DPAFU sensations	Never	Sometimes	Often
Changes to feelings and emotions *continued*			
Not caring about your actions or behaviour		X	
Feeling like an observer of yourself		X	
Problems with your thinking processes			
Finding it difficult to concentrate			X
Feeling like your mind has 'gone blank'		X	
Experiencing thoughts that are speeded up and confused	X		
Having significant problems remembering everyday things	X		
Feeling detached from memories		X	
Having difficulty picturing things in your mind's eye	X		
Struggling to take in new information		X	
Finding yourself repeatedly absorbed in thoughts about the meaning of life and existence		X	

Main DPAFU sensations	Never	Sometimes	Often
Unusual physical and perceptual sensations			
The world around you appears unreal or artificial			X
Physical numbness in parts, or all, of your body		X	
Feelings of weightlessness or hollowness		X	
Losing your sense of taste, touch or smell	X		
Objects around you appearing smaller than they really are	X		
Objects around you appearing larger than they really are	X		
Experiencing distortions to sounds (including your own voice)		X	
The world around you appears less colourful than it really is		X	
Objects and the world around you appear flat or two-dimensional	X		
Objects seeming not to be solid	X		
Feeling detached from your own reflection when looking in a mirror		X	
Feeling as if time has been stopped, slowed down or speeded up			X

If your responses to the statements above are mainly 'sometimes' or 'often', we think this book can make a useful contribution to your efforts to overcome DPAFU. Your answers will show which DPAFU sensations are specific to you. This information will come in useful later when you start to use the CBT strategies we describe in subsequent chapters.

There are also several rating scales used mostly in research to quantify symptoms and track changes with treatment. One scale designed specifically for DPAFU is the Cambridge Depersonalisation Scale (see Appendix I on page 251), which rates the frequency and duration of a range of DPAFU symptoms over the past six months. It is useful if you want to compare the frequency and duration of your symptoms to other people.

In order to score it, total up your responses for both the frequency and duration of all 29 symptoms. A score of 70 or above is associated with a clinical diagnosis of depersonalisation/derealisation disorder. If you score highly on this and want to seek treatment, it might be useful to take along a copy of your completed questionnaire to your GP.

Diagnosing DPAFU

Depersonalisation and derealisation are described in the American handbook of psychiatric conditions, the *Diagnostic and Statistical Manual of the American Psychiatric Association*, Version 5 (2013), known as *DSM-5* for short.

According to *DSM-5*, a diagnosis of depersonalisation/derealisation disorder is made when the following four criteria are met:

1. Where there are repeated episodes of either depersonalisation and/or derealisation, or the symptoms are constant;
2. You know that these experiences are just a strange feeling that you are having and not actually the case;
3. These symptoms are very distressing to you and impact on your ability to function;
4. The depersonalisation/derealisation is not simply an aspect of a different mental health problem (such as panic or depression) but is independent from other diagnoses.

The tenth revision of the World Health Organization's *International Classification of Diseases* (*ICD-10*), an alternative handbook that is used widely by clinicians in Europe for diagnosis, describes depersonalisation/derealisation syndrome as feeling as if you are not really here, or distant from your 'inner self'. Your behaviour and responses may feel as if you are simply 'acting a part' and not genuine; and you may feel detached from your emotions.

As with *DSM-5*, according to *ICD-10*, the affected person needs to realise that their DPAFU only reflects their feelings about the world – and not the way the world really is. Depersonalisation disorder is only diagnosed if the person has this as their main problem and not merely as a part of another problem, such as depression.

If the descriptions above appear to fit with how you have been feeling and/or you do not already have the diagnosis of DPAFU, it may be useful for your future treatment to see your GP and discuss these symptoms. You may wish to take this section of the book along with you. Unfortunately, many of the people we see report that their GP knew very little about their condition and we know that it is not unusual to be misdiagnosed with other conditions. Your GP may want to refer you to a psychiatrist to gain a better understanding of your problems if they are having a significant effect on you.

Can DPAFU occur alongside other mental health problems, too?

DPAFU can occur on its own or alongside a wide range of other mental health problems. These can include agora-phobia (where people feel too frightened to leave their home), or Obsessive-Compulsive Disorder (where people are plagued by intrusive thoughts; for example, the belief that they are dirty or contaminated, and have a compulsion to act on them, in this instance by constantly washing their hands). It can occur with health anxiety (also known as hypo-chondriasis), where people have continual worries about developing a disease despite medical reassurance that they are well; social anxiety, where people are very frightened of being with other people in everyday social situations; and with people who experience excessive worrying.

The sensations of DPAFU are particularly common in people who have panic attacks, with up to 34 per cent of people reporting DPAFU during their attacks. DPAFU is also often associated with people who have depression or continually low mood, and DPAFU sensations can also occur during, and immediately following, a very traumatic experience such as a road traffic accident or a natural disaster.

Sometimes people with DPAFU express concerns that their experiences might lead to other severe and enduring mental health problems such as schizophrenia or psychosis, which involve very different sensations, i.e. hallucinations and delusions. There is no evidence that persistent depersonalisation, in which people describe their experience using the crucial words 'as if', can cause schizophrenia or any other psychotic illness.

Depersonalisation can also be a symptom of neurological conditions such as temporal lobe epilepsy and migraine headaches. As a rule, this kind of depersonalisation is fleeting and associated with other, very different symptoms such as seizures and complete loss of consciousness.

There are a few more situations that can lead to DPAFU. People who have recently been bereaved often experience many of the symptoms of DPAFU. However, these symptoms tend to disappear within four to six weeks, although they can occasionally last longer. Some people also experience depersonalisation when under the influence of hallucinogenic drugs such as cannabis, ketamine or Ecstasy and they start to have unusual experiences or feel very 'speeded up'. Most commonly of all, though, people report short-lived states of depersonalisation when tired, jet-lagged, under severe stress or after an intense emotional experience.

If, while reading this book, you become aware that in addition to having DPAFU you have other psychological symptoms, we would urge you to go along to your GP and seek further help. On the other hand, you may conclude that what you have experienced is not as worrying or as serious as you had feared initially and feel that there is no need for additional help.

How common is DPAFU?

You might be very surprised to discover just how common the sensations of DPAFU are. Indeed, when members of the public are surveyed, the clear majority report that they have experienced DPAFU for brief periods of time. One study found that just over 70 per cent of people reported experiencing DPAFU at some point in their life. It is more common in younger rather than older adults. Another recent random telephone survey in the USA found that nearly a quarter of people questioned have had brief periods of DPAFU during the last year alone. Luckily, more severe DPAFU is less common. Nevertheless, a survey of people in south London, again randomly selected but then interviewed face-to-face, found that up to 2 per cent had DPAFU that was severe enough to be causing distress and significantly affecting their lives. These figures are equivalent to those for other common mental health problems such as Obsessive-Compulsive Disorder (OCD).

The figures increase when the interviews involve people who have mental health problems or have been through traumatic events. For example, up to two-thirds of people who survived life-threatening danger stated that they had DPAFU at the time of their trauma. In addition, those who have diagnoses of depression, anxiety or other mental health difficulties report high rates of DPAFU alongside their other symptoms. Some of the highest rates of DPAFU are in those people who have anxiety problems, especially those who experience panic attacks.

Overall, the results of these various surveys show that DPAFU is not rare. Temporary sensations of DPAFU are widespread in the general population. More severe DPAFU is much less common but still as common as some other well-known conditions, such as OCD.

Is Depersonalisation/derealisation disorder new?

Here's a quote from someone with depersonalisation:

'Even though I am surrounded by all that can render life happy and agreeable, in me the faculties of enjoyment and sensation are wanting or have become physical impossibilities . . . something is between me and the enjoyments of life. My existence is incomplete . . . the functions and acts of ordinary life still remain to me but in every one of them there is something lacking . . . each of my senses, each part of my proper self is as if it were separated from me and can no longer afford

me any sensation . . . it seems to me as if there was a wall between me and the external world.'

What might surprise you about this quote is that although it could be by someone describing their symptoms today, it was written by someone called Griesinger in 1845! Descriptions of depersonalisation and feelings of unreality started to appear in medical books and articles in the early nineteenth century, several decades before the condition was given a name. The term *derealisation* was coined by an Irish psychiatrist, Edward Mapother, who was working at the Maudsley Hospital between the wars. If you are interested in reading more about the history of depersonalisation and derealisation, the books by Dr Mauricio Sierra and Dr Daphne Simeon provide good accounts, and some classic historical books and articles are listed in the Further Information section at the end of the book.

Is there a typical DPAFU pattern?

There is no single type of person who experiences DPAFU, nor is there a set pattern for the way the condition arises or develops. However, studies have looked at large numbers of people reporting recurring or chronic DPAFU and have found some general trends. First, equal numbers of men and women seem to experience DPAFU, which differs from anxiety and depression, which tend to be much more common in women. People often first experience DPAFU in the period from their late teens to their mid-twenties, although there are significant numbers who report their first experience much later than this.

Second, there seem to be three main ways in which sensations of DPAFU first start. Some people describe a sudden onset; i.e. one day it just started, like a switch being flicked. The sensations then remain at roughly the same severity over time. Others mention that they started with short periods of DPAFU that became longer until the DPAFU became continual (i.e. present all the time) or recurrent (i.e. coming back after periods of being absent). Lastly, some people feel that they have always had some DPAFU since a young age, although they were perhaps unaware of this until a later date.

Around 75 per cent of people with continual or recurrent DPAFU experience a sense of unreality about both themselves and the world around them (in other words, both depersonalisation and derealisation). Around 20 per cent experience just depersonalisation and the remaining 5 per cent just derealisation.

In the next chapter, we present case studies of people affected by DPAFU. They illustrate the different patterns of DPAFU and the impact these experiences can have on someone's life.

2

DPAFU case studies

This chapter presents the stories of five people dealing with DPAFU. Their experiences and their backgrounds are all very different. The first person, Anna, had always been a shy person and her problems with DPAFU started soon after arriving at college, when she felt more socially anxious. Michael believed his DPAFU started after illicit drug-taking. Patrick's DPAFU was triggered during a traumatic childhood. Our fourth person, Mina, believed that DPAFU started for no apparent reason. Alexi, whose story is the last featured here, had experienced DPAFU for most of his life, and only became aware of it through listening to a radio programme.

As you'll see from these descriptions, DPAFU affects people in a variety of ways. Maybe you identify with something in these accounts? It may be that you're able to identify with one case more than another, or that you feel that aspects from all the case studies are relevant to you. If you feel that you have nothing in common with any of the cases, you may wish to read the diagnostic criteria (see page 11) and check whether a diagnosis of DPAFU is the right one for you.

Anna

Anna described herself as a shy child who remembered hiding behind her mother's skirt when meeting new people. She was close to her mother and brother but wary of her father, who developed depression when she was young after he lost his business. He could be unpredictable and shout at family members when irritable. Her parents divorced when she was at primary school and this made her feel different from her peers as most of her friends had parents who were still together. She became increasingly anxious with other people, especially if she perceived herself as inferior to them, but had a small group of friends to whom she felt close. She wet the bed until she was aged nine.

In her teenage years, her mother remarried and the family moved to another part of the country at the time Anna moved from school to college for her A-levels. She desperately missed her old friends and found it hard to make new ones after the move. She also felt as if she had lost her sense of security as so much had changed in terms of home, school and location. She gradually started to feel detached and cut off from her emotions and surroundings.

These feelings of DPAFU increased over time and became something that was constantly with her, although they varied in severity. The symptoms were always worse when she had to attend a social event. At these times, she would feel alienated from others and find it hard to talk as she was worried that what she said would not make sense or that her mind would go blank if she was asked a question. She also felt very self-conscious that her DPAFU was obvious to everyone else as she felt her facial expression became blank and unresponsive. She tended to avoid going to events as much as possible but, if she did, she would try to cover her symptoms by keeping quiet and leave as soon as possible.

These problems had been with her for around ten years by the time she was seen in the clinic. She had been prescribed medication for her anxiety by another psychiatrist that she wanted to reduce. With the help of the clinic, she gradually reduced her medication without withdrawal symptoms and learnt ways of managing her anxiety in social situations. She recognised that she had unhelpful thoughts in these situations about what others thought of her and learnt to challenge these and replace them with more helpful thoughts. She also learnt ways to ground herself in the moment and prevent the DPAFU from increasing.

At the end of therapy, Anna still had symptoms but at a lower level than previously. She felt better able to manage these so they didn't interfere with her life and was able to feel more confident around others. She had also experienced some moments when the DPAFU disappeared completely and this gave her hope about eventually recovering fully.

Michael

Michael is a 35-year-old man. He had a happy and loving family, although his mother was quite anxious and his father somewhat distant. His parents were both high achievers and had successful careers. He did well at secondary school and was a popular and able pupil, gaining good grades. However, he had a brief period of bullying that made him feel like an outsider. He went to university to study business. He had a good social life and a wide circle of friends.

One night at a party he took some Ecstasy and later smoked some cannabis (something he had done in the past but not often). But this time he noticed something different about the quality of the experience. He had an overwhelming sense of fear and panic, and desperately wanted the drugs out of his system. He remembers feeling 'spaced out and detached' and felt as if he suddenly saw the world in a completely different way, which he described as his 'Matrix moment'. He went to bed to sleep it off but when he woke the next day he still felt 'odd'. The drugs did not appear to have affected any of his friends in quite the same way. He wondered if the drugs had been spiked or if they had caused some sort of brain damage. He became increasingly aware over the next few months of feeling 'not right'. He had weird visual sensations of a dulling of brightness. It felt as if he was watching life on a video screen. When he looked in the mirror, he was unsure of who he saw in the reflection. On an intellectual level, he knew it was himself but, on an emotional level, it did not feel like him. Things no longer appeared to bother him, and he felt as if he had no emotion at all – 'just nothing; it was like being emotionally numb'.

Michael became very anxious about the meaning of his symptoms. He believed that, if he told someone how he was feeling, they would think he was 'really' mad and he was afraid that he might be experiencing the early symptoms of schizophrenia. However, in the end, Michael went to his college GP, who reassured him it wasn't schizophrenia, and eventually the symptoms faded away. However, he was always concerned that the symptoms might return and he would experience brief episodes of DPAFU when under stress.

When he was thirty, he was offered his dream job but, on starting, he began to experience daily episodes of DPAFU and decided he needed to get help to cope with this and was referred to the Depersonalisation Disorder Service by his GP. Here, he was offered a course of CBT and was able to engage fully with this intervention; he found it helped him to understand the causes and triggers for his symptoms. He began to recognise that his fear of the DPAFU episodes made them worse and was able gradually to learn techniques and strategies to manage these. Over time, the episodes reduced in frequency until they eventually stopped. He has not had any symptoms of DPAFU apart from very transient symptoms for the past five years and is now happily married and continuing to do well in his work.

Patrick

Patrick came from a large family and described a very difficult upbringing. His parents frequently argued and Patrick witnessed them fighting and would try to intervene. His father would physically punish Patrick over the slightest mistake and Patrick felt under constant threat of violence. His mother was critical of him and he felt unloved by her. He felt at his happiest when he was at school, where he was sporty and popular. However, he would feel a sense of dread walking home every day, not knowing what the atmosphere would be like when he got in. During the beatings from his father, he would not be aware of the pain and he felt detached from the event almost as if it was happening to someone else. This had been going on for as long as he could remember.

Aged thirteen, there was a particularly bad argument between his parents during which his father threatened harm to the family and Patrick felt very frightened. That night, he remembers going to bed feeling as if he could not cope with the stress anymore. The next morning, he woke up and his room looked different and everything seemed as if in a dream. He felt as if he no longer existed and his body felt numb. He went to school as normal and didn't tell anyone. Initially, it seemed quite helpful as he didn't feel so upset about what was happening at home but the feeling persisted and started to affect other areas of his life, too. Eventually, he went to see his GP. She thought he was depressed and started him on antidepressants, but these made his DPAFU symptoms worse.

Over the next few years, he tried many different types of medications but nothing ever took away the odd feelings he had and he felt no one really understood or could help. He left home as soon as he was able, moved away and started working. He always struggled with relationships and was only able to maintain these for a few months at a time. He found it hard to trust other people and could feel irritable if he felt others were taking advantage of him. He found it hard to relax, was tense and had frequent headaches. He admitted to drinking alcohol to help him cope with his DPAFU but the amount he was drinking had steadily increased over time. It was only through an Internet search that he found out about depersonalisation and went back to his psychiatrist to ask for specific help with this. His medication was reviewed and a different combination helped reduce the symptoms. He also started talking therapy, where his therapist explained how his DPAFU seemed to have been triggered by the inescapable stress he was under from the beatings and the fear of violence. Therapy focused on helping him make links between his childhood traumas and his DPAFU. After each session, his DPAFU seemed a bit better. He started a new relationship and gradually began to put his past trauma behind him. He still had some symptoms of DPAFU but realised that it would take some time to recover from this and hoped that he would continue to improve after therapy had stopped.

Mina

Mina described herself as a normal child who had a happy childhood. She grew up in a small town in a rural area. She said that she felt close to her parents, particularly her mother. She had a younger sister and brother. As the oldest, she had a lot of responsibility for helping in the house and with her siblings. Her parents were not very sociable and were quite religious. She felt they were strict, didn't like her to go out and emphasised her academic achievement. She did well at school and, after college, she built a successful career in management. She had a good relationship with her boyfriend and was planning her wedding. All was going well in life until, when Mina was 27, her mother developed a terminal illness. She moved back home to help her father cope and nursed her mother until she died. As planned, Mina then married and moved to the other side of town with her new husband. They spent the next couple of years renovating the new house and set up a business together. They would have described themselves as a happy newly-wed couple with a bright future ahead of them.

Then, out of the blue, despite everything going well for her, she noticed a strange feeling when in the company of others. She said it was like being an observer on the outside and looking in. She felt disconnected from other people, including her husband, at these times. She then began to have doubts about whether people that she knew liked her, or whether they felt sorry for her, or only liked her because of her husband.

She began to dwell on her childhood and how lonely and isolated she had felt. Mina began to avoid social gatherings, including her beloved art classes. She became aware that on some days the strange feelings she experienced when others were present began to happen when she was alone. She felt detached from herself and, in fact, said that she no longer knew who she was. At times, she felt as if she would 'disappear' and she would pinch herself because the pain made her feel more real. Familiar places and locations took on an unreal quality. For instance, when driving she felt as if she was experiencing the world through a sheet of glass – she felt cut off from the outside world. She felt that she had no control over her actions and that she had become almost robotic. Her voice did not sound like her own and her hands sometimes appeared to distort in size and image. She believed that she had gone completely mad. But then the next day the sensations would pass, or she would not be aware of them, and things would feel better.

Over a period of a year things got better until no sensations of DPAFU were present. Then, out of the blue, the sensations returned and remained constant. Mina tried to make sense of what was happening to her. There did not appear to be any logical reason why the symptoms should return now. Mina had found out about our unit from the Internet and asked her GP to refer her. She didn't want to take any medication, but undertook a course of CBT. During the treatment, she began to have 'flashes' of reality where very briefly all of her symptoms disappeared. These episodes of reality were enough to reassure her that eventually she would feel well enough to be able to live life as she had hoped and expected. One year on, Mina is free from the sensations of DPAFU but remains reluctant to think of herself as cured.

Alexi

Alexi is a 56-year-old man. After listening to a radio programme, he realised that the description of DPAFU matched perfectly how he had felt all his life. He had been aware of always feeling a bit detached from other people and himself, and places often had an unreal quality to them. In fact, he said that he was 'disconnected' from everything, including himself.

He attributed his feelings to having moved around the world a lot as a child when his father was in the military, and that he had not really formed any 'connections'. But having felt this way for as long as he could remember, he really did not have anything to compare it with. He believed that other people experienced things differently from him, but again had no way of knowing for sure. He felt that he was only 'half living life'. Alexi often felt very low in mood, especially when he thought about the love he had for his wife and children. For him, his love was false because, while he could say on an intellectual level that he loved them, he never felt it emotionally. Life really did feel like it was just a process of going through the motions. He had tried in the past to talk to his wife about how he felt, but she always became upset when he spoke of his 'lack' of feelings for her and their family. He made a conscious decision not to talk about it any further. For Alexi, life was 'one big act'. He said that he knew on a mental level what to do, what to say and how he was supposed to feel, but he never truly 'felt' it. He described himself as being 'numb' inside. He felt that because of his DPAFU, he had not achieved his potential as he had always remained in a 'comfort zone' with the same job, which he found dull.

Following a referral to the unit, he began a combination of CBT and antidepressant medication to help him manage his low mood. During treatment, he became aware of aspects of his life that were 'unrewarding' and 'unfulfilling'. Towards the end of therapy, he decided he would change direction in his work. Instead of working in local government, he chose to work in a less well-paid job for a local charity that he found more interesting.

Six months later, Alexi returned to the unit. He said that he continued to experience sensations of 'emotional numbness' but somehow it was more bearable. His feeling of DPAFU continued to a lesser degree. He believed that the sensations he experienced had less of an impact on his life.

is this unit a place I could actually go to/stay at/recieve treatment from?

3

What causes DPAFU?

Our extensive contact with people who have experienced DPAFU through our clinic and research unit has led to our understanding of DPAFU as a response that is triggered in situations that are perceived by the person as overwhelming, threatening and inescapable. This may happen in response to a sudden event (for example, a bad drug experience or a panic attack) or it may build up over time as events accumulate. Because of the range of people who experience DPAFU, it appears that this is probably an innate response that can be triggered in anyone, given certain circumstances. In this chapter, we will look at our understanding of DPAFU from psychological and brain research.

There are a couple of metaphors that can be helpful to illustrate what seems to happen when DPAFU starts suddenly. One way to think about it is like when an electrical system becomes overloaded – like one of those extension cables with multiple sockets – into which more and more electrical items are plugged in until, eventually, the fuse cuts out. Another useful metaphor is that of an airbag in a car that is activated when the car is about to crash. In both these examples, the fuse or airbag acts to protect the appliance or person in the car from greater harm. In a similar way, it seems that the purpose of DPAFU is to shut down our systems of reality, emotions, thought processes, perception and physical sensations to help us disconnect from what is overwhelming us. This gives rise to the sense of unreality and distance from ourselves and the world that is the fundamental characteristic of DPAFU, as well as buffering us from emotions or physical sensations.

In the short term, this shutdown of human emotional responses may be adaptive and helpful. Imagine, for example, someone involved in a very traumatic, life-threatening incident, such as a natural disaster or a road traffic accident. In this situation, a person may feel so terrified and overwhelmed that they are unable to escape. Imagine, instead, what would happen if they were able to become 'emotionally numb' for a short period. This might be much more helpful. Rather than becoming overwhelmed and unable to function, they would be able to act calmly and leave the situation. However, they may also have a sense of unreality and feel as though they are in a dream, or acting on autopilot both during the experience and for some time afterwards.

You have probably heard about the anxiety 'fight or flight' response to a threatening situation. When we are in a situation of danger, our body prepares us to either attack to defend ourselves (the 'fight' response), or to run away (the 'flight' response). Our body will produce chemicals, such as adrenalin, causing our heart to beat faster and our breathing to be more rapid to increase the oxygen in our blood to give us the sudden energy we need.

However, there is a third common response to threat called the 'freeze' response. This is like the way that some animals might 'play dead' when threatened by a predator. Humans faced with threat can also freeze and this makes them unable to move or react. This is accompanied by a physiological drop (rather than the fight/flight increase) in arousal levels. Some theorists see DPAFU as part of the freeze response to threat in humans. This explanation may make more sense to you if you don't feel that your DPAFU is linked to overt signs of anxiety, as you may be responding to a shutdown or 'freezing' of emotions instead. We think that this 'protective' depersonalisation response was intended by nature to be brief, and for it to last only for the duration of the perceived threat (as in the above example of a life-threatening trauma).

People with DPAFU may have experienced traumatic events that trigger a sudden onset of DPAFU (such as with Patrick), including sudden experiences which an individual might perceive as highly upsetting even if others do not find similar experiences to be traumatic. This is because people differ in how such events impact on them, due to their individual temperament or personal history. In this way, the severity of distress in response to an event is highly personal.

Similarly, people who have a bad response to taking street drugs can have a very frightening experience and this can trigger the DPAFU, too. This was what happened in the case of Michael, one of our case studies. There are also some people, such as Mina, for whom no specific trigger can be identified.

For most people, DPAFU appears to be triggered spontaneously and automatically. However, some people say they were aware that things were becoming overwhelming and wanted to find a way to 'switch off'.

Not everyone reports their DPAFU starting suddenly. In many people, there may instead have been an accumulation of stressful events that led to a triggering of DPAFU to shut off from the overwhelming impact of these experiences. These events may include relationship problems, bullying, work stress or a mix of different problems that all happened within a relatively short period. There may also have been mental health problems such as in the case of Anna, where increasing anxiety or low mood has triggered the DPAFU. Lastly, there are some who, like Alexi, feel that a sense of detachment and lack of emotional response to life has been part of them from as young as they can remember, although it may not be until later in life that they realise this.

Physical explanations: What does the brain have to do with it?

As mentioned earlier, DPAFU appears to represent the activity of a protective *'reflex of the mind'*, or an automatic response, which inhibits the 'emotional' brain in order to protect the individual from extreme levels of anxiety that can hamper our ability to cope with threatening situations.

It is possible to measure brain activation while a person is trying to do various tasks such as looking at emotional images. This shows which bits of the brain are active during such tasks. Recent brain-imaging findings show that a group of brain structures known as the 'limbic system' (also known as the 'emotional brain' and made up of parts of the temporal lobes and deep structures in the front and centre of the brain all connected in a kind of circuit) play an important role in labelling the things with emotional significance. This 'emotional tag' influences the type of emotions we experience in response to situations, objects and people around us, and so provides an emotional context for the way we perceive and experience things. So, in addition to knowing or recognising the things we see or hear around us (knowing that this object in front of me is a tree, a person, a telephone, etc.), we also have an emotional sense about the things around us (I like this object; I recognise this person; that thing frightens me, etc.). This, in turn, determines our feelings of being part of the world, and the way we experience reality. Any disruption in this process could lead to a significant change in the way we experience ourselves and our surroundings – it could, in other words, lead to feelings of unreality.

Brain-imaging studies have shown that people with depersonalisation disorder do not show the usual level of activation in the emotional brain when they look at unpleasant pictures. Likewise, the bodily responses that indicate emotional arousal (an example would be sweating) are unusually small and slow in people with depersonalisation. Some work has also suggested that the hormones that are usually released into the bloodstream in response to stress (such as cortisol) are also reduced in people with depersonalisation – although not all laboratories find this pattern. All in all, this evidence seems to suggest that people with depersonalisation disorder have an oversensitive emotion-suppressing system. This may be because this was used early on in their lives, or because it was triggered by stress or a drug. Or maybe some people are just born this way. No one really knows.

Psychological explanations: What does the mind have to do with it?

In the previous section, we looked at how and why DPAFU tends to be triggered and at the range of reasons and ways this might happen. However, although these examples might help us understand why DPAFU starts, it doesn't explain why for many people the understandable short-term response to feeling overwhelmed becomes persistent and continues long after the triggering situation has passed. We don't know for sure why this happens but psychological theories can provide some good answers.

One possibility is that when someone has experienced DPAFU once, even very briefly, it may be that this results in a lowering of the level needed to trigger this response again. So DPAFU can become triggered more easily in subsequent situations of stress. This would help explain why some people have a pattern of intermittent episodes of DPAFU that become more frequent and longer over time.

There are also some people who have a sudden onset in adulthood, but then recall transient brief periods when they may have felt the same as a child.

For those people who describe always having some DPAFU, it may be that they had adversities as children or were more temperamentally sensitive to experiencing DPAFU. In this way, DPAFU could have become a habitual pattern of reacting to stressful events to the extent that it became almost part of their personality.

Another explanation as to why DPAFU may continue is that the symptoms are so unpleasant and frightening that they themselves become the trigger for them to remain. In other words, the person becomes so anxious and worried about the imminent threat of DPAFU that they remain highly stressed and so the DPAFU persists. This is similar to what happens with people who have panic attacks. The panic attack is so horrible, with physical sensations such as heart palpitations, sweating, dizziness and such high levels of fear that the person often thinks that they are about to die. After experiencing one panic attack, the person often lives in dread of it happening again and starts to make changes to their life to prevent this. However, the worry and stress about the possibility of having another panic attack ironically is likely to increase the chances of it happening again. In this way, a one-off panic attack can develop into the more chronic panic disorder, with repeated episodes. This is what is called in psychological terms a 'vicious cycle'.

Something similar may happen with DPAFU, too. A chronic fear of having another episode of DPAFU, or of the DPAFU becoming worse, can lead to an increase in the stress that might have triggered it in the first place. In this way, what started as a helpful response to overwhelming feelings becomes persistent and chronic.

Many people with DPAFU have worrying and upsetting thoughts about what their DPAFU may mean or how it will affect the future. People often have worries that they might have damaged their brain in some way (particularly if their DPAFU was triggered when taking drugs), that they might be 'going mad', developing schizophrenia or some other 'catastrophic' thought. Although it is entirely under-standable to have these worries given the suddenness with which the symptoms may have started, how strange the experiences of DPAFU might be and how they may seem to be neurological in nature, these thoughts will increase your sense of danger and stress and won't help to alleviate your DPAFU.

DPAFU does not lead on to the development of other serious mental illnesses such as schizophrenia. However, sadly, most people with DPAFU aren't told this soon enough after the onset of their symptoms to reassure them, or they may continue to harbour some concerns despite reassurances because they don't feel confident in the person giving them the information. This is where in-formation from specialist clinics such as ours, where we have seen literally hundreds of people with DPAFU, can really help as people can feel more confident that we know our facts.

Linking body and mind

We've seen how what happens in the brain may lead to the sensations that are associated with DPAFU – i.e. feeling cut off emotionally. We've also looked at psychological factors, such as the worry about the DPAFU leading to these sensations becoming problematic for us. In this section, we'll briefly summarise how the body (physical factors) and mind (thoughts) can interact in general and how this relates to DPAFU.

As we've seen, the power of thought can be tremendous and can directly affect our bodily sensations. For instance, imagine a scenario where you think about a hypothetical negative situation, perhaps taking an exam or driving test. Just sitting and thinking about that situation can trigger physiological and emotional responses – such as increased heart rate, sweating, anxiety, etc. – as if the situation were real rather than hypothetical. Your mind has the power to directly influence your physical sensations. As we have noted in the case of DPAFU, this can lead to increased sensations of feeling unreal, cut off and spaced out. For example, if any person were to look in the mirror for a long period of time and think intensely about their reflection, this is likely to trigger the sensations associated with DPAFU. This is just the same as the way thinking about an impending exam or test will lead to physical sensations of anxiety and stress. As we have seen, what happens next is very important. Continuing to focus on the exam will increase the physiological sensations of anxiety and stress, just as continuing to think about and look at your reflection can lead to an increased sensation of feeling cut off or spaced out.

So far, we have explored how our thoughts and interpretations can affect our physiological and emotional responses. But we have also seen that this is a two-way process. Just as some people may start out with increased physical sensations of anxiety or depression, the same is true of the sensations related to DPAFU. As we have seen, some people with DPAFU may have an oversensitive emotion-suppressing system in the brain. We don't know why this is the case and it could result from either genetic or environmental factors. However, we also know that the way we think can influence the way the brain reacts. In fact, our thoughts, actions and experiences are so powerful that they can modify our actual brain structures even when we're adults. The interaction between the mind and brain is very complex, and we know that the brain is very changeable. For instance, one scientific study shows that twelve people who learned to juggle over three months changed the structure and shape of their brain.

In summary, just as the body can affect the mind, so, too, can the mind have an impact on the body. Both physical and psychological explanations for DPAFU are important and interact with each other. Psychological approaches can be combined with medication or other treatments, and such combinations are usually the best option for people who have more severe symptoms. Using psychological approaches does not mean that there is nothing physical or physiological (i.e. relating to the body) about DPAFU.

In fact, separating 'physical' and 'mental' sensations is old-fashioned and often unhelpful. This means that even if you believe strongly that your DPAFU has a physical explanation, working with your thoughts and behaviour using the CBT techniques we describe in this book is likely to have a positive impact on your physical symptoms of DPAFU.

4

Frequently asked questions

Can people fully recover from depersonalisation/derealisation disorder?

Yes. People can make full recoveries without having any significant symptoms of DPAFU ever again. Others may have mild symptoms that come back from time to time when they are under stress, but they don't worry about it anymore as they know it will pass. One person who had very severe DPAFU and recovered described his later, transient DPAFU as like having a headache – it might be unpleasant and make his day a bit more difficult, but it was no more than that and he knew it wouldn't last long. He had simply lost the fear of the symptoms and this meant he could continue to function.

Many people recover without any medical or therapeutic intervention. When you listen to these accounts, what they repeatedly say is that they gradually learned to accept and cope with the DPAFU and started to get on with their life again. In doing this, the DFAPU stopped being an obstacle and they started to pay it less and less attention. This process made the DPAFU less significant in their life and they started to notice times when they were completely unaware of it. This might have caused them to notice it again in the short term! But in the longer term, this process of coping and carrying on with one's life seems to allow the DPAFU to fade away into the background and gradually, over time, to disappear. For others, getting help through therapy and/or medication might be needed to facilitate this process. Self-help books such as this are also a great benefit to many people in their recovery.

Recovery can mean different things to different people. Much as we'd all love to be able to guarantee that everyone will make a complete recovery and never feel DPAFU ever again – not even briefly – we are not able to promise this. Hoping for this type of complete 'cure' for DPAFU could be compared to someone wanting to never have a common cold again. It's likely to lead to disappointment and frustration. It's more realistic, and helpful, to accept that the DPAFU might recur, and that you can manage it until it gets better again. Recovery is on a continuum, from a complete 'cure' to having a tiny bit of progress, with lots of scope for improvement in the middle. Recovery can mean that your DPAFU is less intense, less distressing and/or causes less interference with your everyday functioning. Any one of these is an improvement, and that's what's important to focus on.

Does the length of time you've had DPAFU make a difference to whether you can recover?

What we've found in our clinic is that most people who

have had DPAFU for a long time have not received the correct help, which may involve specialist intervention, to enable their recovery. Many have stories that include one or more of the following factors which have delayed recovery:

- They did not seek help because they were unaware that DPAFU was a definable problem or that there was any treatment for it;
- They waited a long time to obtain a correct diagnosis as clinicians didn't recognise their symptoms as DPAFU;
- They were misdiagnosed with other problems (such as anxiety or depression);
- They were diagnosed with DPAFU but their clinicians focused on other related issues and didn't directly address their DPAFU;
- They were told that there was no treatment for DPAFU;
- Their clinicians were not experienced in working with DPAFU.

All the above are sadly very common and will impact on the length of time someone may experience DPAFU. One of the areas we are keen to focus on is raising awareness of DPAFU in both public and professional spheres to increase knowledge so people can get better help faster.

If someone has had DPAFU for a long time this doesn't mean that they are less likely to recover, but it may take a bit longer. Associated beliefs and behaviours may have become more embedded and need more time and work to change. For example, people who have had DPAFU for a longer time may have developed a sense of hopelessness about recovery, which may lead them to give up on inter-ventions before they have seen any benefit. However, we recognise that that another form of help may be more bene-ficial to them or that trying again at another time may be more effective. Giving hope and encouragement is vitally important to enabling recovery. In short, change is possible no matter how long the DPAFU has been experienced.

Because so many people have asked us about recovery, we have made a short film about recovery from DPAFU with six people we have seen in our clinic who offer their direct experience of living with DPAFU and who have felt improvement in different ways. To access the film, use the following URL: www.youtube.com/watch?v=GWyidaGt eGg&feature=youtu.be

Is DPAFU very rare?

In an earlier section on how widespread DPAFU is, we talked about how surveys of the condition show that it is actually very common as a brief experience, and that even the more severe symptoms that would be diagnosable as depersonalisation/derealisation disorder are as common as more widely understood mental health conditions such as OCD. It seems as if for a long time the myth that DPAFU is very rare has persisted in clinical settings and, as a result, many people are diagnosed with more common problems such as depression and anxiety and their DPAFU is over-looked. Lack of training for clinicians in recognising the symptoms is partly to blame for this, as well as the difficulty that people having the symptoms have in describing what they are experiencing. This mix of a person struggling to explain their experiences, combined with a lack of recognition from clinicians, has undoubtedly led to many a missed diagnosis. We hope that better training and awareness will help with this difficulty.

I believe my DPAFU is biological in origin, so how can a talking therapy such as CBT help?

Even if you think your DPAFU has a completely biological cause, our emotional, cognitive and behavioural responses can make things better or worse. An Eastern Philosophy metaphor called the Double Arrow illustrates this well. In this metaphor, if you were to be hit by an arrow, you would experience a sensation of pain, but we tend to make things worse by adding a 'second arrow' of our own, which is our evaluation of the experience; i.e. this is pain, it is unpleasant, I don't like it, etc. In the case of DPAFU, the symptoms themselves are difficult enough to deal with, as I'm sure you'll agree. Although understandable, adding emotions (such as anger, sadness and fear), thought processes such as worry and rumination, and behaviours such as symptom checking and avoidance, are likely to add to the original symptoms (or the 'first arrow') and make the overall problem a lot bigger. CBT can help you to identify how your responses may be adding to your difficulties and help you to find more effective ways of dealing with your problem to minimise any possible exacerbation from your reactions. Completing your Personal DPAFU Pattern in the next section will help you to see the ways you might be reacting that may be unhelpful and if there are ways you might be able to cope better.

For now, there isn't a purely biological explanation and treatment for DPAFU, although that's not to say these may be found in the future. In the meantime, CBT can help to ensure that we find the most effective way to manage what may indeed be a biological problem. This is like other forms of physical health problems, such as diabetes and asthma, where there is no defined 'cure' but, with effective management, people can live a valued life with minimal interference.

I've been told by clinicians that DPAFU is just anxiety or just a symptom of another mental health condition – is this true?

Although DPAFU is often closely linked with anxiety and other mental health conditions, such as depression, it is a discrete phenomenon and can occur independently of other problems. The diagnosis of depersonalisation/derealisation disorder has existed for a long time and indicates that, in psychiatric terms, this is a separate condition. Other problems may still co-exist at the same time; just as it is entirely possible to have two physical health conditions at the same time (a headache and a broken ankle, for example), it is also possible to have two mental health conditions simultaneously. One of the skills of a clinician is to be able to distinguish different problems from each other to guide effective treatment.

The key feature of DPAFU that is uniquely different to other mental health conditions is the sense of unreality reported by those who experience it. If clinicians hear people talking about feeling '*as if*' they don't exist or are in a dream, this should prompt them to consider depersonalisation/derealisation disorder as a diagnosis. As mentioned earlier, the '*as if*' quality of this experience – in other words, knowing that something is not right with your perception – helps clinicians distinguish DPAFU from delusional disorders and hallucinations.

Many people with DPAFU report anxiety in their personal history as well as around the onset of their DPAFU. However, the DPAFU can then become dominant and symptoms of anxiety may disappear along with other emotions due to the emotional numbing that happens. Sometimes anxiety and low mood remain but the person with DPAFU feels disconnected from these even though intellectually they know they still experience them. Some people only experience DPAFU within the context of high anxiety, such as a panic attack and, in this case, it is simpler to diagnose this as panic disorder rather than give both diagnoses, as treatment for the panic should resolve the DPAFU as well.

Sometimes, DPAFU is diagnosed as depression. This is often because the emotional numbing of DPAFU can sound very similar to how people with depression talk about feeling unable to experience positive emotions. What is somewhat different in depersonalisation/derealisation disorder is that often the person is emotionally numb to both positive (as in depression) and negative emotions, or feels detached from these. Also, those with depression don't usually report a sense of unreality and this can also help to distinguish the two conditions.

My DPAFU started after I had taken street drugs . . . could I have permanently damaged my brain in some way?

The good news is that there is no evidence of any permanent brain damage in people with DPAFU from the numerous research studies that have been carried out. Most people with DPAFU who have had a brain scan of some sort have entirely normal results and there is nothing that indicates DPAFU from their scans. Many people whose DPAFU started following taking illicit drugs regret their actions and often blame themselves. However, since many people experience DPAFU who have never taken street drugs, the drugs are likely to be only one factor. Indeed, our team of researchers conducted a comparison study between those whose DPAFU started after drug-taking and a group who had never taken drugs and found no significant differences in their symptoms of DPAFU, which supports the view that street drugs alone are unlikely to be the sole cause.

Why has there been so little research into DPAFU?

The lack of research into DPAFU is regrettable. The main reason for this seems to be the myth that it is a very rare condition, which as the statistics show is not true. However, if something is viewed as obscure then it is difficult to get funding to carry out research. Applying for research funding is a competitive process and funding organisations understandably will want to allocate their money to the places where it will have most impact. Similarly, drug companies won't want to invest in finding medications for a condition where they believe that they might not be able to get a return on their efforts. Raising awareness of how common symptoms of DPAFU are is the first step to overturning this lack of research funding.

5

The CBT approach

Cognitive Behavioural Therapy (CBT) or Cognitive Therapy (CT) is a type of talking therapy that has been found to be very effective at treating a wide range of problems, including anxiety, depression, low self-esteem, anger, trauma, eating problems and relationship difficulties. CBT and CT come from the same origins – namely an American psychiatrist called Professor Aaron T. Beck, who worked to develop a talking therapy for depression in the late 1960s. CBT is usually carried out by healthcare professionals such as clinical psychologists, nurses or counsellors who have undergone recognised training in this form of therapy. CBT has certain characteristics that distinguish it from other forms of talking therapies:

- CBT is relatively **short** in duration, usually lasting between 6 and 20 sessions.
- The initial focus is on the '**here and now**'. In other words, therapy typically does not dwell on past events but focuses on solving the problems you have right now. However, longer-term CBT can also address the history of the current problems and work to resolve this, too.

- You work in **collaboration** with your therapist, forming a 'team' in which both of you are equal partners. Your therapist will be knowledgeable about CBT but you are the expert on you!
- CBT is **educational** and aims to teach you **skills** that will enable you to eventually become your own therapist.
- In CBT you take an **active** approach to solving your own problems. Therapy is not something that is 'done' to you.
- It is based on **scientific principles**, and you are like a scientist testing out theories and hypotheses based on your thoughts and behaviours.

How does CBT work?

CBT looks at how five different systems interact with each other. These systems are:

1. **Cognitive:** thoughts, beliefs, meanings, images, attention and memory
2. **Emotional:** how you feel or your moods
3. **Behavioural:** what you do more or less of, things you avoid
4. **Physical:** how you feel in your body such as pain, tiredness
5. **Environmental:** situations, relationships, work, home

Two American therapists who are experts in CBT, Doctors

Padesky and Greenberger, have incorporated these different systems into their Five Systems Model, which has proved very helpful for CBT. Figure 5.1 illustrates how this works.

The idea is that at any given moment these five systems are all interacting with each other. The four systems of cognition, emotion, behaviour and physical sensations are linked to each other. In addition, each of these four systems also interacts with the outside environment (shown in the diagram within a circle).

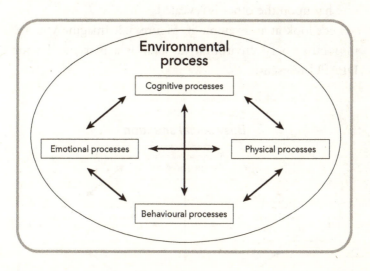

Figure 5.1
The Five Systems Model – Greenberger & Padesky (1995)

If you look at Figure 5.1, you will see that the arrows between each of the systems are double-ended. This is because each of the systems has an impact on each other in both directions. For example, your thoughts or cognitions can affect your behaviour, but so, too, can your behaviour affect your thoughts, and so on.

DPAFU affects each of these five systems, and so a therapeutic approach that includes each of these systems is likely to be helpful. CBT therapy follows this approach and is focused on identifying and understanding your problems and how they affect your mood, thoughts and behaviour in day-to-day life. The relationship between your moods, thoughts and behaviours is then explored and the impact one has upon the other is revealed.

Let's look at an example in Figure 5.2. Imagine you are in a busy social environment, such as a party, and your DPAFU worsens:

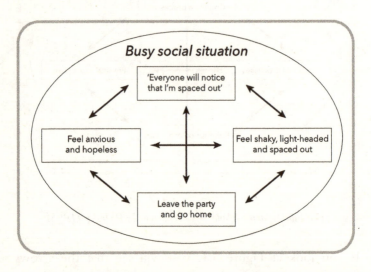

Figure 5.2
DPAFU example of the Five Systems Model

You might have *thoughts or cognitions*, such as 'Everyone will notice that I'm spaced out.' This may affect your *emotions*, such as making you anxious and hopeless. This may have the effect of making you notice your *bodily reactions* of being shaky and light-headed. In turn, this may change your *behaviour* – you may decide to leave the party and go home. Although this may make you feel better in the short term, it is likely you'll feel down and demoralised by having to leave. It's also likely that next time you're invited to a party you'll remember this upsetting event and it'll make you feel anxious that it might be repeated. You may decide that it is safer to just not go to another party. In this way, your problems can increase unless you tackle this pattern. As you can see from this example, a chain of events is set in motion with each element feeding back into all the other elements and making each of these worse in turn.

So how does CBT help in all of this?

The five systems concept is helpful in two main ways. First, once you learn to distinguish each component (e.g. emotions such as 'sad' from thoughts such as 'no one likes me') you can start to understand what is happening to you. This understanding will make your experience seem less overwhelming and confusing. Second, if all five systems are interacting with each other, changing one of the interacting systems will cause a change in all the other components. For example, just by changing your thoughts can influence your emotions, your physical sensations, your behaviour and how you interact with the environment.

Using the example given in Figure 5.2 on page 52, think about what would happen if you were able to replace the unhelpful thought 'Everyone will notice that I'm spaced out,' with a more helpful thought, such as 'Even though I am experiencing some sensations of DPAFU, I know that this is not noticeable to other people.' How would this affect how you feel? Do you think you would feel less anxious and hopeless? Do you think that your physical sensations might improve? Do you think you might be able to stay at the party instead of giving up and going home? Do you think that you might interact differently with people at the party?

The aim of CBT is to recognise, challenge and change the negative or unhelpful patterns or cycles of thoughts and/or behaviours. By doing so, you can change how you feel emotionally and physically, and how you interact with your environment. The following chapters will explain how you can apply these techniques to your experience of DPAFU.

Because of the very nature of this type of therapy, it is an ideal form of treatment for 'self-management' or 'self-help'. The book becomes your therapist. It can guide you through the process of solving your own DPAFU-related problems. It can also help you plan your own treatment. We think that, by following the steps we set out in this book, you'll learn to understand and, in time, overcome your DPAFU.

However, if, after reading through this book and trying out the exercises for yourself, you feel that you need more than a self-help guide to CBT, your GP will probably be the best person to approach. Your GP can refer you to a therapist who works within the NHS. This treatment will be free. Alternatively, you could opt for private treatment. The British Association for Behavioural and Cognitive Psychotherapies (BABCP) or the British Psychological Society (BPS) websites will be able to provide you with the name of an accredited therapist in your local area (see the section on Further Information for useful addresses). However, as the clinician you speak to may not be aware of DPAFU, you may want to take this book along with you to your appointment as it may help them learn more about the problem and direct them towards more information.

Summary

Hopefully by now, this book has helped you to recognise that experiences of DPAFU are common and, although they are unpleasant, upsetting and feel as if they interfere with your ability to function as well as you'd like, they do not indicate any severe or permanent damage – to your brain, for example – or that they will develop into other mental illnesses, such as schizophrenia. You will have learnt that DPAFU is usually triggered in response to feeling overwhelming emotions and appears to be a 'switching off' mechanism that can happen to anyone given the right circumstances. DPAFU experiences are often only temporary but, in some people, they can last longer and finding out what has contributed to your DPAFU and what might be keeping it going will help you to recover from it.

PART TWO

OVERCOMING DPAFU

Introduction

In Part 1 of this book, we looked at DPAFU in general terms – what it is, who gets it, what tends to trigger it and what might keep it going. We also outlined what CBT is and how it might help. In Part 2, we will help you apply this knowledge to your own personal situation and symptoms. We'll start with setting your personal goals for recovery. We'll then help you build a picture of what might have led to the onset of your DPAFU as well as what might be keeping it going. It's important to start here, as this deeper understanding of what might have triggered your DPAFU will highlight the specific areas you need to change.

Later sections will help you to tackle each of these problem areas with useful strategies and tips. These include keeping a diary to help you notice any fluctuations in the severity of your DPAFU to maximise activities that help and minimise those that don't. We'll look at ways of coping with DPAFU by using 'grounding', breathing and relaxation strategies to help you feel more connected and in the present moment. Cognitive techniques will bring awareness to your thoughts and thinking patterns to change those that are unhelpful to be more helpful. Finally, we will look at how patterns of behaviour might also be affecting your DPAFU.

We'll see what we can learn from people who have naturally recovered from DPAFU and how you can maintain hope even if you've had DPAFU for some time. Other therapy approaches, such as mindfulness, can be helpful with DPAFU, so we've included a section on these, too, as well as information on the best types of medication for DPAFU. We'll talk about some of the new treatments which are still in the development stages but that might be effective in treating DPAFU in the future.

Finally, as people with DPAFU often have other problems, such as anxiety and depression, we'll touch on some CBT techniques to help with these, too.

6

Setting personal goals for your recovery

It's a good idea at this point to think about how you'll know when you feel better and when things have changed. Often people say that their goal for self-help or treatment is simply to not have the DPAFU anymore and to never have it again. In other words, a complete 'cure'. Although this is completely understandable, we recommend that you do *not* have this absolute goal for recovery. There are several reasons for this. The first of these is that it can set up high expectations, which, if they don't happen, or are slow to happen, can be demoralising and leave you feeling hopeless. Having a 'no DPAFU ever' goal also sets up a struggle or battle with the symptoms, which might create its own pressure and might serve to perpetuate the stress you are under and so maintain your DPAFU. An image to demonstrate this comes from Acceptance and Commitment Therapy (ACT). What happens when you try to push a balloon under the water? That's right – it struggles to get to the surface again. In fact, the more you push the balloon under the water, the harder it 'fights back' with you. It can be a surprisingly difficult and exhausting game to play.

A similar struggle can happen when you try to push away your DPAFU. It's likely that the harder you struggle to get rid of it, the harder it will push back. We know, from listening and learning from people who have recovered from DPAFU, that change starts to happen when they learn to accept and tolerate their DPAFU. It is then that the symptoms start to become less of a problem for them. This is like deciding to let the balloon bob about on the surface of the water and discovering that this is much easier than struggling to push it away! The DPAFU is there but the person with it isn't caught up in the struggle with it and so can get on with their life instead. It seems that this approach enables the DPAFU to fade into the background and, for some people, the DPAFU gradually disappears.

Our suggestion that you 'accept' the unpleasant, frightening and distressing DPAFU might sound ridiculous, impossible and make you feel angry, as if we don't understand how difficult this suggestion is for you. But this is not a passive acceptance or a giving up. It's actually a very challenging and radical attitude to take. We are suggesting that if you can let go of, at least some of, the struggle with the DPAFU symptoms, then it might make your recovery easier. We are proposing that *as best you can*, you try to carry on with, live with and accept that, *for the moment*, you have DPAFU, despite how difficult that thought may be. Allowing the symptoms simply to be there enables you to not have your life taken up with the struggle of trying to get rid of them. Or to go back to the balloon analogy, the huge effort of trying to keep the balloon under the water.

Of course, we would love for you all to make a full and complete lifetime recovery, but this may not be possible. It is analogous to wanting never to have another headache or cold again and, for this reason, we recommend that you set personal goals for overcoming DPAFU that are relatively modest. It is far better to be pleasantly surprised by how much things have changed than to set expectations too high and feel disappointed. You can also see it as a process where you might set some initial goals and you can recalibrate them again later if you are able to achieve the earlier ones. As the saying goes, a journey of a thousand miles begins with one step.

From values to goals

Acceptance and Commitment Therapy (ACT), mentioned earlier, also emphasises the role of action based on our life values. Values are what is most meaningful to you in your life, that define who you are, or want to be, as a person. They enrich our life and give us a sense of self-respect and of living our life well. Values are things that you continue to work towards during your life and can't simply tick off as 'done'. Examples of values might be being kind to others, trying your best, appreciating what you have. Goals, on the other hand, are steps along the way to a particular value. So, if your value is 'being kind to others', then helping your neighbour fix their fence would be a goal that would fit with your values, too.

To help identify what your values are, look at the following areas and rate the importance of each of them to you from 0 = not important at all, to 10 = extremely important to me. Then think about how things have been for you recently and rate how much you have been able to meet your values using the same scale from 0–10.

Valued area of life	Importance to me 0–10	How much I have met this value recently? 0–10
Friends	9	4
Family	6	6
Intimate relationships	9	10
Work	8	10
Education and learning	7	8
Parenting, grandparenting	N/A	N/A
Leisure and fun	8	6
Community and society	2	2
Spirituality	6	2
Physical health and well-being	5	2
Mental well-being	9	8
Creativity	8.5	0

Now, have a look to see which areas you rate as most important to you but which have the largest discrepancy in the scores. In other words, which ones are you finding the hardest to match your current actions with your values? These are the areas on which to focus most of your attention.

Once you've identified your values where you are not achieving what you would like, this can help you set some goals in these areas.

Often, people simply say when asked about their goals for recovery that they want to 'feel better', but this is too vague and impersonal, and it doesn't fully explain what 'feeling better' means for you. The more specific you can be, the more targeted you can be and the more likely you are to know when you get there. There are several tips for setting personal recovery goals. First, you need to think about *what* changes to aspects of your life would show you that things were better. It's a good idea to phrase these in a positive way (such as 'more of' something rather than 'less of' something). You also need to identify 'benchmarks' that show how *much* things have changed. For example, your goal may be: 'I would like to feel more emotional connection with my family' or 'I would like to feel more real'.

Next, you need to consider exactly how you'll know when this has happened. How will you know when you are feeling 'real'? It's tempting to believe you'll just know, but if our goals are based on feelings alone this can be difficult to judge, as our feelings can change from day to day, or even from hour to hour. It's better, therefore, to base your goals on what you can *do*, in terms of your behaviour, rather than your feelings, as behaviour changes provide a more concrete and sustainable measurement of progress and change.

For a start, try to list your answers to this statement:

I would know that my DPAFU was better if I was able to do the following:

_____

_____

_____

_____

These may be things you *can't* do now (or struggle to do now); things you might be *doing differently* if your DPAFU was better; or something *others would see* you doing that you can't do now or that you'd be doing differently.

Try to make your goals as 'SMART' as possible. This means that they should be:

- **S**pecific (so you know exactly what the goal is)
- **M**easurable (so you can measure change)
- **A**chievable (so you don't set yourself up to fail)
- **R**ealistic (so that it is within your capabilities or possibilities)
- **T**ime limited (so that it does not go on indefinitely)

So, rather than say, 'I would be going out more,' making this specific might be: 'I'd go out with my friends three nights a week.' This would also be measurable if you kept note of how many times you did it every week. But is this achievable? Is it realistic to do this three times a week? What if your friends were not available? Can you afford this? It might be better to set it at a much more manageable level to begin with so you have a feeling of success, which will motivate you to keep going, rather than set the bar too high initially, not achieve it and then risk feeling like you've failed. When you break a problem down into smaller units or steps, things appear more manageable. We'd always recommend you start small and build your confidence gradually. Another tip is to set some goals for different areas of your life, such as work/study goals; goals with family or friends; as well as things you might do on your own.

When you've set some goals, then rate yourself as to how difficult that would be for you to do now, on a scale of 0–10, where 0 is not at all difficult and 10 is extremely difficult. This is your own personal scale as it applies to you, so don't worry about how anyone else would find this, but be sure to use the same scale throughout these exercises. Where you would like to be will become part of your *goals*. Don't automatically go for 10 as your final goal. Instead, try to be realistic, and settle on a number that would be 'good enough'. Think about how much of an issue the specific problem is for you. Sometimes, we have to learn to accept experiences or sensations that we would rather not have, and so we 'manage' rather than 'cure' them. Think, too, about the impact the sensations or symptoms associated with DPAFU have on your everyday life. Identify those activities that you would like to do more of, and those you would like to stop avoiding.

Here are some of the most common reasons for finding goal-setting difficult:

- Goals are far too big and unrealistic.
- Goals are not specific enough. For instance, a goal to go out more needs to be more clearly defined. It's best to be as specific as possible – i.e. go out twice a week for two hours, once to the pub and once to the cinema.
- There is no form of measurement at the beginning from which to monitor change.
- Goals are too easy to achieve and so aren't a challenge.
- There's no time frame, which can sometimes lead to a feeling of drifting along so you may lose a sense of direction. This can, in turn, reduce your motivation and self-discipline.

Before we move on to the next section, have a think about the following question: *When is a problem not a problem?* The answer is: *When you say so*! People vary in the ways they perceive problems in life. If you feel 'a bit odd' but still go to work, and then go out with friends in the evening, then feeling a bit odd does not stop you from leading a normal day-to-day life. In this instance, feeling odd is not a problem. But if when you feel a bit odd you take the day off work, stay in bed and worry about the way you feel, it becomes a problem. This is especially so if it happens often, or if you believe the odd feeling is the result of something you've done (like take a drug), or if it appeared to come out of the blue and you spent time trying to figure out why it happened. In each of these situations, you would begin to experience the sensations as problematic. It's always worth having another think about each of the sensations you've defined as being problematic. At this stage, you may want to redefine the different levels at which DPAFU affects you, what exactly each problem stops you from doing and how it operates.

7

Understanding your personal DPAFU pattern

When you go to see a psychologist or CBT therapist, they are likely to ask you about your personal history from when you were young, about what was happening to you when your DPAFU started and about how you react to it now. The reason for these questions is so they can see what may have led to the problem and what might be keeping it going. In this section, we'll help you do this for yourself so that you can understand better why this may have happened to *you*.

A useful template for this is called the '5 Ps Model'. This is because there are five factors that all start with the letter P. It looks at the following:

1. **Predisposing factors**: these are the temperamental, psychological, social, environmental, physical and cultural factors that may have led you to have a greater susceptibility to developing DPAFU.
2. **Precipitating factors**: these are the things that may have happened in the period immediately leading up

to your DPAFU starting. This period may last for days or weeks, or there may have been an accumulation of factors in the months leading up to the DPAFU being triggered.

3. **Present problems**: this will include your DPAFU, but there may well be other problems, too, in your life now. If so, they can be included here.

4. **Perpetuating factors**: Sometimes the way we think, feel and behave in response to our present problems – although understandable – might inadvertently make the problem worse or cause it to last longer. To change these problems, it is important to identify these and make changes. This is where CBT can really help.

5. **Protective factors:** These are things that help the problem or prevent it from getting worse. Identifying and enhancing these will help protect us from the present problems.

Some of these factors are in the past (predisposing and precipitating), and some are current (present problems, perpetuating and protective). To give you an idea of how you can build up your own individual DPAFU pattern, have a look at the following worksheet template that you will complete at the end of reaching this chapter with each of the factors that apply to you. In the next section, you will find guidance on how to fill in each of the key areas, and there are some examples of completed worksheets for you to look at as well.

My Personal DPAFU Pattern

Predisposing factors

....

....

....

Precipitating factors

....

....

....

Thoughts/Images

....

....

....

....

Thought processes

....

....

....

Present problems

....

Behaviours

....

....

....

....

Emotions

....

....

....

....

Bodily sensations

....

....

....

....

Protective factors

....

....

....

Creating your personal DPAFU 5Ps pattern

It will be helpful for you to create your own 5 Ps model. In this section, we will look at each of the Ps in turn and provide a checklist to help you to identify what might fit with your own history and current problems. We'll start with the Ps from the past (predisposing and precipitating) and then move on to the current Ps (present problems, perpetuating and protective). Hopefully, the checklists will help you to identify what may have happened to you. We can only include here some of the more common factors, so we've left space for you to add your own in case they are not already on the list.

1. Potential predisposing factors

These are things that might have affected your likelihood of developing DPAFU from your earliest days. Have a look at the checklist and tick any that apply to you.

Potential predisposing factors	Applies to me?
Difficult family environment growing up	
Criticism or hostility from a parent or caregiver	
Emotional coldness, indifference or rejection from a parent or caregiver	
Family arguments	
Difficult relationships with siblings	
Parental separation/divorce	

Childhood bereavements	
Childhood trauma	
Childhood physical abuse	
Childhood sexual abuse	
Childhood neglect (e.g. not having sufficient food or clean clothes)	
Parental mental health problems, please specify...	
Parental substance or alcohol misuse	
Bullying within the family or at school	
Feeling an outsider at school	
Childhood shyness/lack of confidence	
Childhood mental health problems (e.g. anxiety or low mood), please specify...	
Childhood physical health problems, please specify...	
Parental physical health problems, please specify...	
Childhood/adolescent drug or alcohol use	
Study or work stress	
Financial stress	
Problems in relationships with boyfriends/girlfriends	
Other problems not listed above (please specify):	

2. Potential precipitating factors

Below is a list of events that might have happened in the period (days, weeks or months) leading up to your DPAFU starting. Have a look at the checklist and tick any that apply to you.

Potential precipitating factors	Applies to me?
Family arguments	
Difficult relationships with parents	
Difficult relationships with siblings	
Parental separation/divorce	
Bereavement	
Adult trauma	
Adult physical assault	
Adult sexual abuse	
Parental mental health problems, please specify………………………………………….................	
Parental substance or alcohol misuse	
Study or work stress	
Bullying at work	
Adult shyness/lack of confidence	
Anxiety problems, please specify…………………………………………..................	

Panic attack	
Depression or low mood	
Other adult mental health problem, please specify..	
Adult physical health problems, please specify..	
Parental physical health problems, please specify..	
Adult drug or alcohol use	
Financial stress	
Problems in relationships with romantic partners	
Separation or divorce	
Losing your home	
Unemployment	
Other problems not listed above (please specify):	

Reviewing your predisposing and precipitating factors

What did you learn from doing this exercise? Were you able to identify factors that may have contributed in the long or short term to your DPAFU starting? Have you had to deal with adversity or trauma? Were there events that were out-side your control that triggered feeling overwhelmed and trapped? Was there a sudden event that caused the DPAFU to start? For many people with DPAFU, this exercise is an eye-opener as they just hadn't realised what may have con-tributed to their DPAFU. Doing this can not only highlight the difficulties so you know what you may have to address but can also encourage you to feel some empathy and com-passion for yourself, especially if you tend to blame yourself for your problems.

For people whose DPAFU started in adulthood, you are likely to have a list of predisposing *and* precipitating types of factors. You may have a long list that applies to you, or just a few significant factors. Did you find any factors that appeared in both lists? If so, these will be par-ticularly important issues for you to address in the rest of the book.

For those of you whose DPAFU started in childhood or adolescence, the predisposing factors may also have been the precipitating triggers, too, in that your DPAFU started early on. If so, then just include the predisposing factors in the template.

3. Present problems

In this section, we're going to look at what problems you have currently. This will include your DPAFU, but are there other things to add to this list, too? Have a look at our checklist and tick any that apply to you.

Present Problems	Applies to me?
Family arguments	
Difficult relationships with parents	
Difficult relationships with siblings	
Bereavement	
Adult trauma	
Adult physical assault	
Adult sexual abuse	
Caring for family members	
Study or work stress	
Bullying at work	
Adult shyness/lack of confidence	
Difficulties in social situations	
Anxiety problems, please specify..	
Panic attacks	
Depression or low mood	
Other adult mental health problem, please specify..	
Physical health problems	
Illicit drug use	
Alcohol use	

Financial stress	
Problems in relationships with romantic partners	
Separation or divorce	
Losing your home	
Unemployment	
Other problems not listed above (please specify):	

4. Perpetuating factors

In this section, we're going to look at some things that may be keeping your DPAFU going so that we can use CBT to help us change some of these. It helps to separate these into different categories similar to those described at the end of Part 1, in the Five Systems Model of Greenberger and Padesky. The reason for separating these out is that we deal with each of these in a different way, which will be covered in later sections. The five categories of potential perpetuating factors are:

Thought content (including images)

Most people with DPAFU will have negative thoughts about their symptoms. Although this is completely under-standable, these thoughts and images are likely to make you feel worse and it is useful therefore to identify your most habitual or upsetting ones and add them to your personal DPAFU pattern.

Typical examples of unhelpful thoughts about DPAFU include:

- 'I'm never going to get better . . .'
- 'This is getting worse . . .'
- 'My DPAFU affects my ability to function properly . . .'
- 'I've damaged my brain in some way . . .'
- 'People notice my DPAFU . . .'
- 'This might develop into schizophrenia . . .'
- 'I'm damaged . . .'
- 'I might disappear or get lost in another reality . . .'
- 'I'm useless . . .'
- 'No one can help me . . .'

You'll notice that all the examples given are in quotation marks. It's best if you can write down your thoughts in this way, just as they appear in your mind, as they will be more accurate and unedited. You may also have helpful thoughts, too. These are good and will make you feel better and we want to keep these! But we don't want to add these in the template as we are creating a list of your *difficulties* here and don't want to mix up the unhelpful and helpful because we only want to change the unhelpful thoughts.

The content of your thoughts might also include images, too. These might be visions of yourself being unable to communicate, looking detached, losing your job, being a patient in a mental health ward, or some other distressing image.

List your most common unhelpful thoughts and images here:

_____

_____

_____

_____

_____

_____

Thought processes

This category is about the patterns of how your mind works, rather than the specific thought content and images as in the previous category.

Examples that might apply to you are things like:

- Difficulty processing information or 'brain fog'
- Memory problems
- Constantly monitoring the severity of your DPAFU
- Concentration difficulties
- Racing thoughts
- Difficulty focusing

- Going over and over things in your mind ('obsessing/ ruminating')
- Worrying about the future
- Getting caught up in philosophical thoughts about the meaning of existence that don't have answers
- Thinking about things from the past ('ruminating')
- Mind going blank

List your most common unhelpful thought processes here:

_____

_____

_____

_____

_____

_____

_____

Unhelpful behaviours

This category of perpetuating factors describes how your problems affect you in terms of your activities or behavioural responses. Are there things that you do more or less because of your DPAFU and the problems you are encountering? Include only unhelpful patterns here.

Typical examples of unhelpful behaviours include:

- Avoiding situations (e.g. crowds, shops)
- Self-medicating with alcohol, drugs or food
- Internet searching for DPAFU 'cures'
- Self-harming
- Seeking reassurance
- Insomnia
- Pretending to be 'normal'
- Escaping situations where you feel worse
- Avoiding social situations
- Staying in bed/indoors
- Excessive distraction (e.g. TV/Internet surfing)

List your most common unhelpful behaviours here:

_____

_____

_____

_____

_____

_____

Distressing emotions

This category of perpetuating factors is for feelings and emotions. These are usually described in one word. You will already have DPAFU in your present problem category, so use this category to describe other emotions you might have.

Try to use words that describe specific emotions, such as in the list below, rather than generic words such as upset or distressed. Also try not to overload your list by using words that are synonyms of others and mean virtually the same thing. So instead of 'frightened, panicky, anxious, worried', which are all very similar to each other, see if you can choose just one that is the best way to describe how you feel.

Typical examples of emotions in those with DPAFU include:

- Anxious
- Overwhelmed
- Stressed
- Sad
- Hopeless
- Angry
- Guilty
- Despairing
- Helpless
- Frustrated

List your most common distressing emotions here:

_____

_____

_____

_____

_____

_____

_____

Bodily sensations

These perpetuating factors describe the physical difficulties that affect your body that you might have associated with your DPAFU and other problems. We're particularly looking for things that will adversely affect your behaviour, emotions and thoughts.

Typical examples of bodily sensations include:

- Fatigue
- Tension
- Dizziness
- Numbness
- Palpitations
- Visual disturbances
- Shortness of breath
- Lethargy
- Agitation

List your most common bodily sensations here:

_____

_____

_____

_____

_____

_____

_____

Protective factors

So far, your personal DPAFU pattern has only included things that are unhelpful, distressing or problematic to you. In this category, you can include things that help you to manage your DPAFU and make you feel better able to cope (even if only temporarily). You can include emotions, thoughts, situations, thought processes, behaviours and physical sensations in this section.

Typical examples of protective factors include:

- Support from friends and family
- Getting a good night's sleep
- Being absorbed in something interesting
- Reminding myself of the good things in life
- Exercise
- Listening to music
- Letting go of worries
- Spiritual beliefs or practices
- Having a relaxing bath
- Medication
- Reading recovery stories
- Eating well
- Talking to others

- Walking in the countryside/enjoying nature
- Pets
- Keeping optimistic about my future
- Keeping calm
- Mindfulness exercises
- Creative activities

List your protective and helpful factors here:

_____

_____

_____

_____

_____

_____

_____

Case Examples of Personal DPAFU patterns

Let's look at worked examples of each of the case studies we discussed in Chapter 2 before you try to complete one for yourself. By summarising the key issues for each person, these DPAFU patterns can highlight what needs to change.

In the same way, your personal DPAFU pattern can help you to work out what needs to change to get better in your own life.

Anna's Personal DPAFU Pattern

Predisposing factors

Shyness

My father's depression, irritability and unpredictable behaviour
Parents' divorce making me feel different from my peers
Social anxiety
Low self-esteem

↓

Precipitating factors

Changes in family set-up (new stepfather)
Moving away from where I grew up
Starting a new school

↙ ↘

Thoughts/Images

'If I say something
it won't make sense'

Image of my
face looking
unresponsive

Thought processes

Worry
Focus on DPAFU

Mind going blank

Present problems

DPAFU
Social anxiety
Low self-esteem

Behaviours

Avoid social events

Keep silent

Leave as soon as
possible

Emotions

Alienated
Anxious
Self-conscious

Bodily sensations

Butterflies in tummy
Shaky
Withdrawal symp-
toms from medication

Protective factors

Support from mother and sister, close friends

Anna

Can you see what may have led Anna to be anxious in social situations? You'll see that for Anna her current worries about what others think of her make her anxious in social situations and increase her DPAFU. What would really help her is for her to approach rather than avoid social situations and to learn ways to manage her anxiety when she's there. For instance, she could then experiment with acting differently, such as trying to speak more and see how others react. This will allow her to test out if her predictions of not making sense happen or are just a worrying thought. Perhaps she can look at photos of herself in these situations to see if her face is as expressionless as it feels to her. She can then build up her confidence and gradually tackle more difficult situations for her. Hopefully, these strategies would help to prevent her DPAFU from increasing in severity at these times, and a boost to her self-esteem more generally might reduce it overall, too.

Michael's Personal DPAFU Pattern

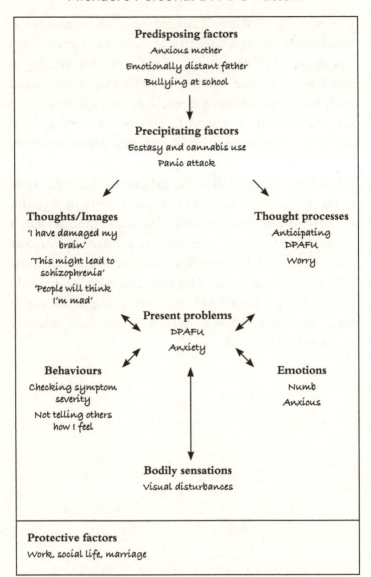

Predisposing factors
Anxious mother
Emotionally distant father
Bullying at school

Precipitating factors
Ecstasy and cannabis use
Panic attack

Thoughts/Images
'I have damaged my brain'
'This might lead to schizophrenia'
'People will think I'm mad'

Thought processes
Anticipating DPAFU
Worry

Present problems
DPAFU
Anxiety

Behaviours
Checking symptom severity
Not telling others how I feel

Emotions
Numb
Anxious

Bodily sensations
Visual disturbances

Protective factors
Work, social life, marriage

Michael

For Michael, it would be helpful for him to understand how his drug-taking has not damaged his brain, to be reassured that DPAFU does not lead to schizophrenia and that others don't see him as mad. This will help reduce his worry, which is interacting to worsen his DPAFU. He can also learn that by anticipating the DPAFU, he is likely to make it more likely to happen because of his anxiety getting worse. Learning that he can manage despite having symptoms and how little people notice of his DPAFU would be useful to him. Grounding strategies to use at moments when he feels an increase of symptoms can help, too.

Patrick's Personal DPAFU Pattern

Predisposing factors

Parental arguments

Physical beatings from father (with transient detachment)

Critical, unloving mother

Feeling under constant threat at home

Precipitating factors

Violent argument between parents

Stress

Feeling unable to cope

Thoughts/Images

'I'm damaged goods'

'No one can help me'

Thought processes

Intrusive memories
of childhood

Ruminating on
current problems

Present problems

DPAFU

Depression

Behaviours

Ending relation-
ships

Wanting to be alone

Misuse of alcohol

Emotions

On guard for danger

Irritable

Lacking in trust

Bodily sensations

Tense

Headaches

Aches and pains

Protective factors

Medication

Patrick

Patrick's DPAFU started during the beatings he received and later became more constant. He doesn't trust other people and is on his guard for signs of danger. These factors are likely to be maintaining a sense of threat, which might be perpetuating the DPAFU. Helping him to see that what happened when he was a child is still currently having an impact on him in this way will allow him to make changes. There *was* danger for him in the past but this danger is not current. His rumination about the past and thoughts that nothing will help him are making him feel depressed. These thoughts can be challenged and more objective, helpful thoughts generated.

Mina's Personal DPAFU Pattern

Predisposing factors

Early responsibility at home

Strict parents

Lonely as a child

High parental expectations

Mother's illness and death

↓

Precipitating factors

Nothing adverse identified

(Perhaps feeling under pressure to do well as adult?)

Thoughts/Images

'Others don't like me'

'I need to be perfect'

'I've gone mad'

Thought processes

Worry about the future

Present problems

DPAFU

Behaviours

Avoid social events

Pinching myself

Reassurance seeking

Emotions

Frustrated

Helpless

Bodily sensations

Not able to feel body weight

Hands appear distorted in size

Protective factors

Intelligent, good job, supportive husband, religious beliefs, artistic

Mina

Mina was initially puzzled as to why she developed DPAFU but, by mapping this out, she could start to see that her parents had high expectations for her, which she had internalised. When everything was going so well for her, there was underlying worry that things might go wrong and that she might fail and only have herself to blame. Learning to be more compassionate and accepting of herself would help her, as well as reducing some of her perfectionistic tendencies.

Alexi's Personal DPAFU Pattern

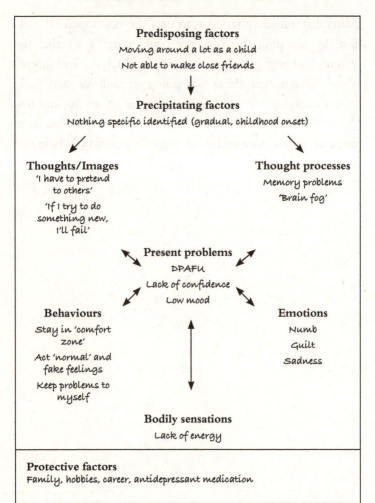

Predisposing factors
Moving around a lot as a child
Not able to make close friends

Precipitating factors
Nothing specific identified (gradual, childhood onset)

Thoughts/Images
'I have to pretend
to others'

'If I try to do
something new,
I'll fail'

Thought processes
Memory problems
'Brain fog'

Present problems
DPAFU
Lack of confidence
Low mood

Behaviours
Stay in 'comfort
zone'

Act 'normal' and
fake feelings

Keep problems to
myself

Emotions
Numb
Guilt
Sadness

Bodily sensations
Lack of energy

Protective factors
Family, hobbies, career, antidepressant medication

Alexi

Alexi could see that he had always been a detached observer of life, which seemed to stem from moving so much as a child where he learnt it was not worthwhile to invest too much as he would have to move on and leave it all behind anyway. Detachment was a way of protecting himself from continual loss. This had led to him leading a safe but dull life and not taking risks. Pretending everything was OK just intensified his sense of being fake and of unreality. He could make some changes to his life and take some calculated risks. He talked more openly to his wife about his problems. Rather than be upset with him, she was pleased that he had shared his feelings with her and felt more able to help him. She told him what a good husband and father he was and this alleviated his guilt and sadness. Together, they decided that he should do something workwise that he felt engaged with and he changed his job. He was more accepting that, for him, managing his DPAFU would be a slow process given that this was almost part of his personality.

Putting your personal DPAFU pattern together

Once you've listed all the possible factors that might have contributed to your DPAFU starting on the checklists above, as well as identified things that might be contributing to keeping it going or making it worse, you can then transfer these on to your 'My Personal DPAFU Pattern' worksheet – either use the template shown earlier on page 72, or create one of your own. This will allow you to see these factors more clearly to help you better understand what might have caused your DPAFU and to identify what needs to change.

TIP: If you have a lot of items in a particular category, you might want to prioritise which of these is the most important. By only adding the most relevant of these to the Personal DPAFU Pattern worksheet, you will be keeping the information as clear and as helpful as possible.

Once you've done this, spend some time reflecting on your pattern. Can you see what might have triggered your DPAFU? Were the triggers mainly external factors, internal factors or a mixture of both? Perhaps whereas previously you attributed it to one thing, you can now see that there were several things that accumulated? For those of you who had an adverse drug reaction, this exercise may have helped you see that there may have been other factors that also contributed to the onset of your DPAFU. Perhaps you were going through a particularly difficult period of your life at that time and there was a combination of things that affected you?

What about the factors that might be contributing to the problem? Are there particular patterns here? Are there things that are both in the past and in the present? Anxiety is a common example of this in that it might be something you've had since childhood, something that was particularly bad when your DPAFU started and something that you still have now. If there are any things that come up repeatedly, then these factors will be important for you to change.

Having completed your Personal DPAFU Pattern, you can now move on to strategies and techniques to help each of these factors in the next sections.

Summary

We have discussed some of the most common predisposing and precipitating factors that trigger DPAFU. We have also looked at some of the perpetuating factors as well as protective factors that help. You have seen how this pattern can be used with our case examples and then completed your Personal DPAFU Pattern. This will enable you to see clearly how there may be unhelpful interactions between your present problems, and perpetuating factors such as thoughts and images, thinking patterns, emotions, physical symptoms and what you do. In the next chapters, you will learn ways of dealing with each of these issues.

8

Keeping a DPAFU diary

Keeping a diary of your DPAFU sensations at the start of the self-help process can be very helpful for several reasons:

- Rating the intensity of your DPAFU sensations at frequent intervals can help you to identify whether there are any fluctuations as well as any patterns to these fluctuations.
- Noting down what you are doing and the severity of your DPAFU can help to show any associations between activities and symptom severity.
- Gaining a better understanding of what affects your DPAFU will give you a greater sense of control. This is because it will enable you to try to modify the situations that cause your DPAFU to worsen and increase the situations that improve it.
- Completing a diary will give an accurate measurement of the frequency and intensity of your DPAFU as it stands now. After you've tried out the techniques we describe in the following sections of the book, you can keep another diary. Then you can compare them to see how your sensations of DPAFU have changed and in what ways.

Before we go on, a word of caution. Keeping a diary of this kind is a staple of CBT treatment for many conditions, especially anxiety and depression, and has been used by thousands of people over the years. We think it can help many people with DPAFU, too. However, by charting your DPAFU severity, you will bring more attention to it and this may increase your awareness of the symptoms. In the short term, this increased focus on your symptoms may make you feel a little bit worse, as instead of distracting yourself and avoiding thinking about the DPAFU, you are instead being asked to focus on it. You may also find this makes you a bit low in mood as you recognise the problems you are currently experiencing.

So why are we asking you to do this? The reasons are that it will give you more insight into what is happening to your DPAFU and more information as to what affects it and therefore how you might start to change it. We are only suggesting that you keep a diary for a week, or two at the most, and believe strongly that the long-term advantages of doing this outweigh any possible short-term disadvantages. If you don't do a diary review, you may miss out on useful information that will be helpful to you.

With these cautions in mind, there are two types of diary we recommend. The first is a diary in which you rate the severity of your DPAFU on an hourly basis. This is useful if your DPAFU is constant and affecting you all, or nearly all, the time. The second type of diary is one for those of you who have intermittent symptoms. In this version, you record the severity of your DPAFU and the situations, thoughts, emotions and behaviours only when you have an episode.

The hourly diary for continual DPAFU

For some of you with DPAFU that is with you continually, you already may be aware of certain situations, times of day, activities and emotional states that affect the severity of your symptoms. Even so, the hourly diary is a useful way to see if you can pin more of these down. You will then be able to gain a clearer understanding of why these fluctuations occur with the subsequent diary analysis.

For others, you may feel like there is little or no variation at all in how you feel. Your DPAFU seems constant and unremitting. For this reason, you may think there is not much to be gained from keeping a diary. However, what we find in most people is that the diary can often detect slight and subtle variations in the DPAFU sensations. These may be difficult to recognise at first but it is worthwhile keeping a diary for a short period to see if you can detect any changes and by carrying out the analysis that we describe here.

You'll find an example of a partly completed diary from Alexi on pages 106 and 107 to show you how the diary might look when it is completed, and you'll find a blank copy for you to fill in in Appendix II on page 266.

You will see that the diary looks rather like a timetable, with the days along the top and the time (in hours) down the side. For each hour, there is a very brief description of what you are doing and a rating of the intensity of your DPAFU, from 0 (indicating none whatsoever) to 10 (indicating the worst your DPAFU has ever been). There are no right or wrong responses to this – just note down whatever score seems most appropriate to describe how you are feeling.

Tips for completing your diary

- Try to keep your description of what you are doing brief so you can fit it into the square, but as specific as possible. So rather than complete a whole day with all entries simply stating 'at work', instead break this down into the specific task you were doing, such as 'in a meeting', 'lunch with colleague', 'checking emails' and so on, as this will give better information to analyse.

- Try as best you can to complete the diary as close to the time of the activity as possible as this will allow you to be more accurate in your DPAFU ratings. If it is too difficult to do this every hour, then try to identify a couple of time points during the day when you can fill in the diary, such as in coffee breaks or lunch. If even this is not possible, then set aside some time in the evening to review your day.

- If completing on paper is difficult for you, make notes – perhaps on your phone – and transfer this to the diary sheet later.

- If you think that you might have problems remembering to complete the diary, pop some reminder notices up around your home or work and keep your diary somewhere to hand or in view to help you remember. Creating alerts on your phone to remind you to fill it in can also help.
- If you miss some time periods and don't feel you can accurately remember the ratings for this, then leave these out and start afresh when you do remember. It's better to have fewer but more accurate ratings.
- If your DPAFU doesn't fluctuate much in intensity, then try using a 0–100 rating instead as this allows you to make more subtle changes in the ratings. You might only notice a change of 1–2 per cent, but this is still worth observing.
- Similarly, if you want to use a 0–10 scale, try using 0.5 scores to create more range.
- If your first week of completion has been typical, then this is likely to provide all the information you need for the analysis. If for some reason it wasn't very typical, then complete the diary for another week to get more data.

Alexi's Hourly DPAFU Diary

Time	Thursday	Friday	Saturday	Sunday
6–7am	Sleep	Sleep	Sleep	Sleep
7–8am	Breakfast DP=2	Breakfast DP=3	Sleep	Sleep
8–9am	Travel to work DP=6	Travel to work (busy) DP=8	Breakfast DP=1	Sleep
9–10am	Paperwork DP=5	Presentation to clients DP=10	Tidy flat DP=2	Read papers DP=1
10–11am	Meeting with boss DP=9	Talk to clients DP=9	Go shopping in town DP=4	Listen to radio DP=1
11–12pm	Meeting with boss DP=8	Finish meeting DP=6	Go shopping in town DP=4	Tidy up DP=1
12–1pm	Work phone calls DP=6	Write report DP=5	Lunch in town DP=4	Drive to parents DP=8
1–2pm	Lunch in the park DP=3	Lunch with a friend DP=4	Get kit together DP=3	Help prepare lunch DP=2
2–3pm	Prepare presentation DP=5	Phone calls DP=5	Football in the park DP=2	Lunch with family DP=3

3–4pm	Prepare presentation DP=6	Paperwork DP=4	Football DP=2	Chat to Dad DP=2
4–5pm	Phone calls DP=5	Plan for next week DP=4	Shower DP=1	Drive home DP=8
5–6pm	Travel home DP=6	Travel home DP=5	In the clubhouse DP=4	
6–7pm	Shop in supermarket DP=8	Shower & get ready DP=2	Go home/change DP=3	
7–8pm	Eat meal DP=3	Meet friends for drinks DP=5	Meet date for a meal DP=8	
8–9pm	Watch TV DP=3	Chat with best friend DP=3	Watch film with date DP=5	
9–10pm	Watch TV DP=1	Talk to new people DP=8	Watch film DP=4	
10–11pm	Read in bed DP=1	Go home DP=4	Drinks in pub with date DP=7	
11–12am	Sleep	Sleep	Home – watch TV DP=3	
12–1am	Sleep	sleep	sleep	

Analysing your diary

The first thing to do when you have completed your diary is to look at the range of scores, from the lowest score to the highest score. For some of you this might be nearly the full range, for others it might only vary a small amount. Once you have done this, you can then separate the scores into the highest scores (when your DPAFU is at its worst), and lowest scores (when your DPAFU is at its best). These will be the most useful scores but you might also want to look at the middle range of scores, too.

When we look at Alexi's diary, we can see that, although he experiences DPAFU all the time, his range of scores is from 1–10; in other words, the intensity of his DPAFU varies significantly depending on his situation and what he is doing. Using the detailed information from his diary we can see the times when his DPAFU is at the lowest, middle and highest points and see if any patterns emerge. One way of doing this is to categorise his activities according to their DPAFU scores. For the range of scores that Alexi has, it makes sense to group these from 1–3, 4–7 and 8–10. We can then simply list out his activities in each of these categories.

High DPAFU activities (scores from 8–10):

- Meeting with boss
- Shopping in supermarket
- Travelling to work (when busy)
- Presentation to clients

- Talking to clients
- Talking to new people (in social situation)
- Meeting date for meal
- Driving

Moderate DPAFU activities (scores from 4–7):

- Paperwork at work
- Travelling to/from work
- Phone calls at work
- Preparing presentation
- Meeting at work
- Meeting friends for a drink in a bar
- Shopping and lunch in town
- Chatting in the clubhouse
- Watching film with date
- Drinking in pub with date

Low DPAFU activities (scores from 0–3):

- Meals at home
- Lunch in the park
- Watching TV
- Reading in bed
- Showering
- Chatting to best friend/father
- Doing housework
- Playing football
- Listening to the radio
- Lunch with family

Tips

If your diary has only a small amount of variation in the scores, use the same method as described with Alexi but with a smaller range in each category. For example, you may only have activities with a score of 5, 6 or 7; or it might even be only 8.5, 9 and 9.5.

If there are no fluctuations whatsoever in your diary, then other techniques we will cover later in the book may be of more use to you.

Reviewing the possible reasons why there are fluctuations in your diary

You can use the table below to look at the reasons why certain activities and situations might have an impact on your DPAFU.

Analysing Possible Reasons for Fluctuating DPAFU Severity

Times when my DPAFU symptoms are at their worst			
DPAFU rating	What I was doing	Possible reasons why	What could I do to change or modify this?

Times when my DPAFU symptoms are at their best			
DPAFU rating	What I was doing	Possible reasons why	What can I learn from this?

Review of Alexi's Diary

Analysing Possible Reasons for Fluctuating DPAFU Severity

Times when my DPAFU symptoms are at their worst			
DPAFU rating	What I was doing	Possible reasons why	What could I do to change or modify this?
8	Meeting boss	Stressed because I felt underprepared	Prepare agenda items in advance. Remind myself about my recent good appraisal
8	Shopping in supermarket	Bright fluorescent lights/lots of people/ noisy	Go at a less busy time/wear tinted lenses to reduce glare
8	Travelling to work when busy	Feel trapped in crowds/dreading the day ahead	Take a quieter route/Go earlier to miss the rush hour/use relaxed breathing and grounding strategies to help reduce anxiety and DPAFU/ notice and challenge my negative thoughts (see later sections of book)/plan something to look forward to during the day
10/9	Presenting/ talking to clients	Worried I might make a mistake	Do a run-through in advance/focus my attention on them and not how I'm feeling

8	Talking to new people	Concerned they will notice my DPAFU	Remind myself that others can't notice my DPAFU
8	On a date	Anxious to make a good impression	Take the pressure off myself by reminding myself it's just a date and not the end of the world. Be kind to myself and try to enjoy the moment
8	Driving	Find this hard with DPAFU	Reassure myself that I'm a good driver

Times when my DPAFU symptoms are at their best			
DPAFU rating	What I was doing	Possible reasons why	What can I learn from this?
3	Meals at home	On my own/ relaxed	If I relax, my DPAFU reduces
3	Lunch in the park	Outside/taking a break from work	Taking short breaks outside helps during the day/ do more activities at lunch such as going for a walk
1–3	Watching TV/ reading in bed	Relaxing, distracted from my symptoms by interesting programme	If I get engrossed in something I don't notice my DPAFU so much. I could try some puzzles to take my mind off things
2	Showering	Water on my skin makes me feel more in my body	Slowing down and noticing sensations helps me
2–3	Chatting to best friend/dad	Feel supported by them	It's good to talk to people who know me

2	Playing football	Takes my mind off my problems/ fun/exercise/ being with my team	Sports are a great distraction and lift my mood. I could join other group activities such as a photography class

When we look at Alexi's DPAFU, we can see that there is a theme in that his symptoms appear to be at their worst in stressful work and social situations. This is especially true when he interacts with new people, groups of people or people who increase his anxiety (such as his boss or having a meal with his date). Crowded and brightly lit environmental situations, such as travelling and supermarket shopping, also increase his DPAFU. Alexi's DPAFU sensations worsen when he drives.

This analysis of what makes his DPAFU worse highlights what areas he can start to make simple changes in first. In the last column, Alexi has already been able to think about some strategies he can try to help reduce the impact of some of these situations on his DPAFU. He appears to have quite a lot of anxiety in social situations and worries about how others might evaluate him and it would therefore be worthwhile for him to learn ways of tackling these feelings. Strategies such as grounding, relaxed breathing and dealing with negative thoughts and self-focused attention will be covered in more detail in later chapters.

However, when he is at work and in social situations where he feels more comfortable, his DPAFU is lower. The lowest levels are when he is quiet at home, experiencing physical sensations such as showering or playing football, or when he is with close family and friends. Alexi has learnt that if he can be more relaxed, take more breaks, reduce his worries, engage in activities and keep his mood lifted then his DPAFU symptoms improve. He can use this information to add these factors more generally into his life.

Reviewing your diary analysis

Once you have completed your diary analysis template, ask yourself some of the following questions:

- What can you learn from your pattern of DPAFU?
- Are there particular situations that always make it worse?
- Do these have specific themes?
- Is your DPAFU worse at a particular time of day or week?
- Is feeling better or worse related to how you are feeling?
- Are there links with anxiety or low mood?
- For each of the worst times, is there anything you can do to modify the situation to make it a bit easier for you (but without avoiding it altogether)?
- What about the better times – are there themes to what helps your DPAFU?
- Is there any way you could transfer learning from some of the better times to some of the more difficult times?

- What are the main things you need to address to make your DPAFU better?
- How can you build on your strengths?

The key thing in reviewing your diary is to see how much you can generalise from it. It is not just a matter of looking at specific situations or activities that make your DPAFU better or worse, but as best you can try to understand *why* in particular these might affect your DPAFU. Looking for themes or underlying reasons will help. You might not automatically know what it is about the situation that is affecting you, but perhaps you can make some educated guesses? What might you say to someone else?

Typical situations that make DPAFU worse are often those that create stress, anxiety or low mood. Situations where you shift your focus of attention to your symptoms are likely to make you feel worse. Negative thoughts are common triggers, too.

Alternatively, being more relaxed, among family and friends, feeling less time pressured or engrossed in something tend to help.

Hopefully, you have learnt some valuable things from your diary-keeping that you can address using the other strategies we will cover in the rest of the book.

The diary for intermittent DPAFU

If your DPAFU is intermittent and comes and goes, you will instead want to complete a different type of diary that records what is happening just before and during your DPAFU episodes. This will help you detect any patterns that may be triggering the symptoms.

Below is a completed example to give you some ideas. We have included a blank diary sheet for you to copy in Appendix II on page 269:

Situation	Thought(s)	Emotion	Behaviours	Sensations
Sitting watching television	It looks unreal What is wrong with me?	Worried	Stop watching TV and check my vision every 5 minutes	My foggy vision is getting worse
Driving in my car	What happens if my derealisation worsens – I will crash the car and I will kill somebody	Anxious	Go home as quickly as I can. I have decided to only drive short journeys from now on, just in case.	My heart rate has gone up. I'm feeling panicky
Talking to my best friend	Why can't I feel emotions? I can't feel affection for my friend anymore	Frustrated, sad	Go to bed and lie awake trying to figure things out.	Emotionally numb

There's no set format to this type of diary so we suggest you try something like the example provided and then adapt it to meet your needs. The essential components are to record what was happening just as the DPAFU started. This should include what you were doing, how you were feeling physically and emotionally, as well as the thoughts you were having and how you reacted to the DPAFU. We have included a blank diary sheet for you to fill in or copy here, and you'll find one in Appendix II at the back of the book, too.

How long you will need to keep up this diary depends on how frequent your episodes are. You will want to get enough information on typical episodes to see if you can detect any patterns. For those of you with episodes that are very infrequent, this may take some weeks.

Once you have the information, you can use the following questions to guide your self-analysis. Can you see if there are any common themes to the situations? Are there particular emotions that trigger or accompany the DPAFU? Are there thoughts that set it off? What do you do in response to the DPAFU? Is this helpful or potentially unhelpful? Once again, patterns that you learn from this diary-keeping will guide what needs to change and will allow you to benefit most from the later sections.

Diary-keeping is a powerful tool. Use it for a specific purpose – e.g. 'I want to see if my sensations differ according to the time of day' – not as an open-ended habit or substitute for living. Although generally helpful, sometimes diaries or journals can become a way of ruminating on problems or difficulties. If you tend to do this, restrict your diary-keeping to the sort of formats recommended above and don't make it a repository of how bad you feel and all that is wrong with the world. If you're worried about becoming obsessed with observing yourself, or if you've recognised that this is a problem you would like to avoid, restrict yourself to a set period of updating and review – say half an hour in the evening.

9

Coping strategies for DPAFU

In this section, we will look at some simple coping strategies to use when your DPAFU is at its worst. These include 'grounding' strategies and imagery, simple breathing techniques and relaxation.

'Grounding' strategies

Grounding strategies are so named because they aim to 'ground' you in the here and now, in the present moment and place, rather than in the past or the future. They are very helpful for people with DPAFU to use when they feel an increasing sense of detachment or unreality to stop these sensations escalating.

Grounding strategies can take several forms. These include: using your surroundings; your senses; words or statements; objects; posture; and images. We discuss each of these in the following pages. We recommend reading through this section to see what you might like to try out for yourself. Grounding strategies need to be personalised as different things work for different people.

There are a couple of overarching tips. Generally, the simpler the strategy, the better. This is because when you are feeling increasingly detached, depersonalised and derealised, you simply don't have the cognitive capabilities to use something complicated. You also need something quick and accessible, so grounding strategies that need nothing apart from what you might have immediately to hand work best. It's also good to have a variety of these so that you don't overuse one strategy so it becomes ineffective over time. The more the merrier applies in the case of grounding strategies! You will also want to practise using these when you are not in most need, ideally for a few minutes every day, to make them effective. Start off when you feel relatively relaxed and have only low-level DPAFU or your DPAFU is not too severe. Then, once you've gained some control over your DPAFU, you can use these techniques to help you when the DPAFU is worse.

Using your surroundings to ground yourself

Look around at your surroundings. Try to notice everything in the most precise detail possible and describe it to yourself. This is best done aloud if you can; otherwise, do it silently in your head. Describe your surroundings by asking yourself questions such as:

- Where am I right now?
- What town am I in?
- What building am I in?
- What day is it?
- What time is it?
- What do I see around me? Describe each object . . .
- What colours are there?
- What shapes can I see?
- What textures do I see around me?
- How bright or dark is it where I am?

Keep asking yourself these questions until you feel fully grounded in time, place and reality.

Grounding using all five senses

You can use each sense to help ground yourself.

Vision

In addition to the strategies described above using your surroundings, you can also use specific pictures or objects to look at. You might want to have some photos on your phone or videos to watch. One client made short video clips of her playing with her pets, which she would play when she was feeling at her worst, and this helped her remember better times and gave her a sense of home. Pictures of beautiful or inspirational places can also work well.

Sound

Listening to music is a common source of support to people. You might like to create your own soundtrack to help you feel grounded. This might have personal significance to you, or be uplifting or peaceful. Again, it is for you to trial what works best for you.

Touch

By using touch as a grounding strategy, you can bring yourself back into your body again. You might find soft, comforting textures help you or, alternatively, textures that are stimulating. One client kept a rough pebble in his pocket and found this helpful to rub when he felt his DPAFU worsening. This brought him back into the present moment.

Taste

The taste of certain foods or drinks may be useful to you, such as peppermint or a strong flavour. Again, it is about having something close to hand, so flavours that you can carry around easily are best.

Smell

Aromas and scents are one of the most powerful of grounding strategies. Our sense of smell is very instinctive and can bring you right into the moment by instantly dispelling any other thoughts. People often choose favourite perfumes, or essential oils such as lavender. Menthol and eucalyptus scents work well, too. You can also still buy old-fashioned 'smelling salts' in pharmacies, which were used in the past when people felt faint. They are very strong-smelling, however, and don't suit everyone, although they work extremely well.

Grounding words or statements

Some people find the use of grounding words or positive statements very helpful. These should aim to make you feel strong, positive and acutely aware of being alive in the moment. Remind yourself of your good qualities, your strengths or the good things in your life. Examples of positive grounding statements might be:

- 'I am strong and I will get through this . . .'
- 'I will succeed if I keep trying . . .'
- 'My family and friends are here to support me . . .'
- 'These feelings will pass . . .'
- 'I will make the most of today . . .'
- 'I am here and I am OK . . .'

Create your own list of words or statements that make you feel positive and grounded. Write these on cards or on your phone so that you can carry them around with you to read to yourself when you start to experience DPAFU. You can even make a recording of yourself saying these statements so you can give yourself an instant 'pep' talk! You might want to include messages from other people, too.

Grounding posture

You may find it helpful to change your physical position if you start to experience DPAFU. Adopting a stance that makes you feel strong and grounded will work best for you. This may be standing up straight, with shoulders back and head held high. It may involve consciously letting go of any tension you feel in your body, keeping your shoulders from hunching and letting your arms and hands relax by your side. Alternatively, you might prefer settling into a comfortable chair and allowing yourself to flop like a rag doll to relieve the feelings of tension. Perhaps stretching to the sky or becoming aware of the weight of your feet on the ground will help to ground you. Try several different postures to see what works best for you.

If you are in a situation where you can't obviously change your position – such as in a meeting at work – you can try FOFBOS. This stands for 'Feet On Floor, Bottom On Seat'. In other words, wherever you are sitting, bring your attention to feeling your feet on the floor. See if you can notice the sensations of touch on the soles of your feet. Picturing roots coming from your feet and spreading into the ground can help you feel even more 'grounded'. Similarly, notice the sensations of touch at the points of contact with what you are sitting on. Can you feel where your legs and bottom touch the chair? Can you feel the chair taking your weight and supporting you? Are there other points of contact such as your arms, back or head? Bringing your awareness to FOFBOS can really help give you a sense of grounding and no one else will notice at all!

Grounding objects

Objects can be useful for giving a sense of grounding and bringing you back to reality. Choose something that has personal significance for you, and that you can easily carry on your person or have to hand. Examples might be a piece of jewellery, your keys, a keyring, a pen, a scarf, a handkerchief, a soft toy, photos of yourself and loved ones, your phone, a business card or a letter. Any of these could work. When you start to feel sensations of DPAFU, use your grounding object to remind you of who you are and where you are.

Grounding images

If you feel overwhelmed by your DPAFU (or any other negative feelings), using visual imagery can be very calming and grounding. Think of a place that brings you a sense of peace and tranquillity. This can be a real place that you know (such as a beach, park or building) or an imaginary place, like a fantasy castle, or floating on a cloud. If it's a real place, choose somewhere that has no negative memories associated with it.

- Shut your eyes and imagine yourself in your 'special place'.
- Take the time to really focus on the details of your surroundings; the more detail you can create, the greater your sense of grounding will be.
- What do you see around you?
- Are you on your own or would you like someone to be there with you? Who would that person be? Would you like a favourite pet or animal to keep you company and/or protect you?
- What are you doing in your special place?
- What can you hear? If you're outside, can you hear nature? If other people are around, are they talking or laughing?
- Can you feel any sensations on your body? Is it warm or cold where you are?
- What smells or tastes do you associate with this place?
- What emotions do you experience when you imagine yourself here?
- Where do you feel those emotions in your body?
- What single word would sum up this special place for you?

Practise your grounding image every day. Try to add more detail each time so that it becomes more and more vivid. The greater the detail and realism, the greater will be your sense of security, calmness and grounding when you visualise it.

Grounding tips

For your grounding to work best, you'll need to practise it regularly. The beauty of grounding techniques is that they are so easy to do, anywhere and at any time. You can close your eyes and use your grounding image while sitting on a bus, hold your grounding object when in a meeting, adopt your grounding posture when in social situations, use your grounding words when you wake up in the morning. In fact, you can ground yourself in your surroundings at any time of the day or night. Practise the strategies before you need them and you'll find they work better when you do!

Simple relaxed breathing

When we become anxious and stressed, our normal breathing patterns can change so that our breathing becomes faster and we take in more oxygen. There's a good reason for this happening, which is part of the 'flight or fight' response we mentioned earlier in the book. What our body is trying to do is to oxygenate our blood so we have more energy for fighting off the danger or to help us run away faster. However, the effects of over-breathing or 'hyperventilating' can be very unpleasant and may contribute to your DPAFU.

Sometimes, if we have been over-breathing for a while we will even have a sensation of our lungs and chest tightening. This is the body trying to restrict the amount of oxygen coming into our lungs. Ironically, if we don't understand this, this can feel more anxiety-provoking as we feel we can't catch our breath! Noticing if we are over-breathing and doing something about it can help us feel calmer and reduce these unpleasant side-effects.

THE OVER-BREATHING TEST

Here's a quick test to see if you might over-breathe when you feel anxious. Write down a list of the symptoms you experience when you feel anxious. Then practise over-breathing for just 1–2 minutes, while timing yourself. To over-breathe, try to pant like a dog that has been running, through your mouth, and as fast as you can. Don't do this for longer than two minutes. Write down the list of sensations you are experiencing now. Compare this to the list you wrote earlier about the symptoms and see if any of the symptoms match. If so, this suggests that over-breathing may be contributing to your difficulties.

What did you notice from the over-breathing test? Did you experience a worsening of your DPAFU? Were you light-headed or dizzy? Did you feel sick or experience symptoms of nausea? Were there any other sensations you noticed? If the answer is yes, you might want to learn how to control your breathing to reduce the effects of over-breathing so you don't add to your difficulties.

Breathe out!

Sometimes, people have been taught that relaxed breathing is about taking 'deep breaths' but, as you can see from the over-breathing exercise, this is likely just to make things worse! As you will have surmised from the above explanation, the key thing you need to do to counter over-breathing is to try to breathe *out* more than you breathe in.

If you become aware that you have been over-breathing, focus your attention on your out-breath. See if you can fully breathe out. Sometimes people find it helps to imagine blowing out candles on a birthday cake; a birthday cake of someone who has a few miles on the clock is particularly helpful! Don't worry about your in-breath as your body will be doing this automatically. Just spend a few minutes focusing on breathing out.

If it helps, you can introduce a count to your out-breath. This helps you to start to lengthen it. However, as with all breathing techniques the trick is to keep relaxed, so don't try to force it and stop if you find you are getting more anxious. Over a few minutes, you might be able to increase the length of the out-breath gradually. In normal breathing, our in- and out-breath should be balanced in length, but when we are anxious or stressed our in-breath is longer. See if you can gradually address this imbalance by lengthening your breathing out.

In yoga, there is an entire set of practices that focus only on breathing ('*pranayama*'). The in-breath is the 'breath of energy' as it brings oxygen into the body; the out-breath is the 'breath of relaxation'. If you want to learn about breathing techniques in more detail, see if you can find a yoga class that will teach you some of these.

Relaxation

Given that anyone with DPAFU is likely to be having a difficult and stressful time, relaxation is extra important. We all need 'down time' in order to let our bodies and minds slow down, rest and recuperate. If, in addition to DPAFU, you also have anxiety and low mood, then you will need to focus more on relaxation as your mental health will make it hard for this to happen naturally. Anxiety can result in physical tension in the body so it is important to counteract this with active relaxation. Practising regular relaxation can help our anxiety levels reduce and come back to a lower baseline level.

Relaxation comes in a variety of guises. You could try exercise, such as walking, swimming or a good aerobic workout. You might prefer to spend some time on a favourite hobby. Experiment to see what works best for you. It might be an activity not traditionally associated with relaxation, such as gardening, cooking, sewing or DIY.

For many people, it helps to use some guided exercises to aid relaxation. There are many available as audio guides or apps. Ideally, you would want to practise these on a regular basis to keep your stress levels within reasonable limits. Regular practice will also mean that when you are more stressed and need the relaxation to be most effective, your body and mind will be used to relaxing and you will find it easier to do.

One of the techniques often used by psychologists and therapists is called Progressive Muscle Relaxation. We've included a guide below so you can practise for yourself. You may find it helpful to record yourself saying these instructions, so you can simply listen to the steps, rather than trying to remember them. Over time, you can learn the routine and can then practise it in your head whenever you need it. At the start, allow yourself some space and time away from everything to get the best chance to relax. Take yourself somewhere quiet, where there will be minimal distractions. Try to allow yourself this little bit of time to devote to your own well-being. Sitting in a comfortable chair or lying on the floor is often best. Lying in bed often leads to falling asleep; although if you are sleep deprived, this might be of benefit. If you have developed peaceful and relaxing grounding imagery from earlier in this section, you can include that in your process to enhance the effect.

PROGRESSIVE RELAXATION

Start by either sitting or lying in a quiet, comfortable room. Make sure you won't be disturbed and that there are no distractions. Keep yourself warm as when you stop moving your body temperature may drop. Close your eyes or, if you prefer to keep them open, softly focus on a fixed point.

Start by noticing the points of contact between your body and the ground. Feel the floor or chair that is supporting you. Let yourself sink into your support and allow gravity to let your muscles relax.

Bring your awareness to your breathing. Without trying to change anything, simply notice your breath in and then your breath out. See if you can follow each breath all the way in and all the way out. Notice the slight pause as the in-breath stops and becomes the out-breath. Notice the out-breath becoming the in-breath. Observe how your body just breathes all on its own without any effort from you. See if you can treat each breath as unique. Notice how your body moves in response to the breath. Is there a part of your body where you notice your breathing most? Is it at your nostrils, in your chest, or your abdomen? Let your awareness settle here and simply watch your body move. Allow yourself to just be here, not trying to do anything else but simply breathe.

Once you have had some time to settle into being here, you can move on to the progressive muscle relaxation. In this you'll focus your attention on each part of your body in turn and notice how it feels. You will then tense up each part of your body for a few seconds, and then relax, letting go of this tension and noticing the difference between the tensing and relaxing sensations.

Start at your toes and feet. Lift your feet from the ground and clench your toes. Hold this tension for a few seconds and then let your feet gently drop to the floor. Notice the sensations of relaxation flow into your feet.

Now lift your left leg slightly and tense the muscles in your leg as you do this. Hold for a few seconds and then let your leg flop down. Notice how your leg feels now as the muscles relax. Now repeat this in your right leg. Pause and notice the feelings of relaxation in both your legs.

Now lift your hips up and tense the muscles in your stomach and buttocks as you hold your body off the ground or chair. Then, relax and let your body lower to your support. Bring your awareness to how this feels.

Repeat in your upper torso, lifting and tensing the muscles in your chest and upper back. Hold for a couple of seconds. Then gently lower and sink into the ground, chair or bed. Let gravity help your muscles relax.

Take a few slow breaths while you are here. Notice how your torso and legs feel now they have relaxed.

Now, lift your left arm up slightly, clench your fist and hold the tension in your muscles, before letting your arm flop to the ground. See if you can notice the sensations of relaxation in your arm when you do this. Repeat with your right arm and hand. Pause and notice the relaxation in your arms, torso and legs.

Next, lift your shoulders towards your ears and hold here. Notice the tension created in your shoulders and neck as you do this. Then let your shoulders relax down as far as you are able. Notice where you might still feel any tension here and spend a moment or two simply breathing and letting go of this as best as you are able.

Now, scrunch up the muscles of your face and hold this for a few seconds. Notice the tension in your facial muscles as you do this. Then let the muscles in your face relax. See if you can let the skin on your face become loose. Bring your awareness to any parts of the face which hold tension and see if you can bring more relaxation to these.

Now, notice the sensations of relaxation throughout your entire body. Enjoy the feelings of letting go and sinking into your support. There is no need for your muscles to do anything so let them be loose and relaxed. Allow your breathing to be slow and relaxed. Take as long as you want to rest here, enjoying the time to look after yourself. You can picture yourself in your special peaceful place while you stay here.

When you finish, take your time to slowly adjust back, roll on to one side and take a few moments before you stand up.

Barriers to relaxation

If you find that you avoid relaxation because you believe it makes your DPAFU worse, you'll need to tackle this problem as it is important that you take time out to relax. Try to identify what it is about relaxation that you don't like or what you are worried about.

Perhaps you find that upsetting thoughts or memories, or images of past traumatic events, come into your mind when you try to relax. If this happens, make a mental note of any ideas and themes that keep occurring so that you can use the strategies we'll cover in the next chapters to deal with them.

Some people with DPAFU find having the time and space to relax heightens their awareness of how they're feeling. When you're relaxing there's little to distract you and so there is a tendency to focus on yourself. As mentioned earlier, the more you notice and look for sensations, the more you'll find. But even if you have found that relaxation has made your DPAFU worse in the past, it's very important that you don't avoid relaxation altogether. Relaxation won't make your DPAFU worse. We all need to relax and, in fact, not allowing yourself to do so may lead to additional problems such as more stress and anxiety. Now that you have a greater understanding of how your thoughts and behaviours can impact on your DPAFU, have another go at relaxation. Perhaps this time, if you realise that it wasn't the relaxation, but rather your heightened self-monitoring that made you more aware of your sensations, you'll have a more positive experience.

Or perhaps you're concerned that you might get feelings of panic. If so, remind yourself to think of yourself as a scientist carrying out an experiment. Scientists start by predicting what might happen in an experiment. The prediction here would be that nothing catastrophic will happen. If you do begin to feel panicky, remind yourself that it is just anxiety. If you're anxious, your heart rate is increased, but that doesn't mean you're going to have a heart attack. Your breathing rate will increase, but that doesn't mean you're going to suffocate. When you increase your breathing, your mouth goes dry. When you're feeling anxious, your blood flow is concentrated between the heart and the brain, which may lead to your hands, feet and limbs feeling tingly or very heavy or numb, or to you experiencing pins and needles. These are the physical reasons why you're having these sensations. When you know what to expect, and what follows in the chain reaction, you'll feel less scared if it happens.

Allow any thoughts to come, rather than fighting them. Instead, just try to observe and be aware of them. After all, they're just thoughts. You can't make your DPAFU worse just by thinking about it, even though you may feel that you can. All that might happen is that you become more aware of the sensations associated with DPAFU. But let these thoughts and sensations come and try not to be frightened. You can't cause a brain tumour, schizophrenia or any form of madness just by thinking about it.

Summary

In this section, we've looked at some ways of coping with your symptoms that will help you to gain some control over them. Grounding strategies aim to help you feel more present in the moment. Simple breathing techniques will help to calm you when you are anxious or stressed and may reduce some of the symptoms that are due to over-breathing. Finally, relaxation can help you to rest and let go of some of the physical tension your body may be holding and give some respite to your mind.

10

Thinking in new ways: changing your thoughts

Some of the most powerful techniques in the CBT toolkit are those that help us to bring an increased awareness to how our thinking can become biased and distorted, as well as ways to deal with unhelpful or negative thoughts. In this section, we will look at the most common thinking errors and how this can affect our DPAFU; learn how to tackle these thoughts and replace them with more balanced and helpful thoughts, by using a technique called a 'Thought Record'. Later in this section, you'll find strategies to deal with unhelpful thinking processes such as self-focused attention, worry and rumination.

Common thinking errors

Professor Aaron T. Beck, who developed CBT, noticed that depressed patients had a particular way of thinking about themselves and others, the world and the future. He observed a tendency towards a negative style of processing information – the glass was always half empty, never half full. He noticed that the negative patterns in thinking styles were very common and often included negative bias or error. These are often referred to as **cognitive distortions.**

In fact, we are all prone to making these errors, even when we don't have any mental health problems, but when we are low in mood, anxious, or have DPAFU, we are likely to do this even more. The list below outlines some of the more common cognitive errors or distortions and how they may appear in people who experience DPAFU. It's unlikely that you have found yourself thinking every one of these thoughts, or even most of them, but you probably have had some of these thoughts at some time or another. See if you can notice which ones are most familiar to you.

- **All-or-Nothing Thinking:** This is when things seem black or white with no in-between. If it's not perfect, then it's a failure; if it's not right, then it must be wrong. '*If my DPAFU is present then I won't enjoy the day.*'
- **Negative Mental Filter:** You single out one negative detail and focus on it at the expense of any positive features. You have a night out and focus on the brief period of time when you felt DPAFU. You then remember the whole evening as a disaster.
- **Fortune-telling:** You predict the future as being negative. '*My DPAFU will only get worse.*'
- **Overgeneralisation:** You make a whole pattern of negatives from just one or two instances. You did

one thing wrong and think that you did everything wrong. '*All my negative feelings are because of DPAFU.*'

- **Catastrophising:** You think that what has happened or what will happen is awful or unbearable. '*My DPAFU will get worse, I will lose my job, my wife will leave me, I will be alone, I will lose my house.*'

- **Labelling:** You use negative labels for yourself (and others) like '*I'm a failure*' or '*I'm useless*' or '*I'm mad*'.

- **Disqualifying the Positive:** Even when you become aware of positives, you find a way to discount them. '*It's not that my DPAFU is better, it's that I don't notice it as much. I did enjoy the pub but my DPAFU spoilt it.*'

- **Exaggeration:** You magnify any mistakes, mishaps or negatives. You speak up at a meeting and don't believe you sounded as you hoped. Then you might think to yourself that everyone thought you were stupid and was laughing at you and you will probably lose your job. Or you think, '*If I go out when my DPAFU is bad everyone will know I've "lost it" and my friends will abandon me.*'

- **Jumping to Conclusions:** You assume that you know what others think or feel about you or your behaviour – you think you are an accurate 'mind-reader'. Or you think you know what will happen in the future, and that you are an accurate 'fortune-teller'. '*If I go out when my DPAFU is bad, everyone will know I feel strange and uncomfortable.*'

- **Personalisation:** If something bad happens, you

assume you were in some way responsible. If something goes wrong at work then you assume it was just down to you and not in any way the department or system that is to blame.

- **'Should' Statements:** These are the rules that you make for yourself. These rules tend to be inflexible and cause personal upset and distress when broken, often leading to feelings of guilt. *'I should never have taken that drug or let stress get the better of me. If I hadn't, then I would not be in this state (DPAFU) now.'*

- **Emotional Reasoning:** Assuming something to be true based on only a feeling. *'I feel so odd this must be the first sign of madness.'* This is one of the most common cognitive errors that people who experience DPAFU are prone to.

- **Blaming:** You focus on someone or some things as the source of your negative feelings or problems. *'My DPAFU is to blame for my partner leaving. My DPAFU stops me from working.'*

This is not an exhaustive list but covers the most common cognitive errors reported by people with DPAFU.

Professor Beck observed that the distortions only became problematic when they occurred too frequently, or when someone experienced a serious incident, such as a trauma or illness. To illustrate the different kind of automatic thoughts that might pop into your head, imagine you're walking down the street and you pass an old friend who does not acknowledge you – what is your first thought?

1. They did not see me
2. They ignored me on purpose
3. They never liked me
4. They must have had other things on their mind

If you believed that numbers 1 or 4 were the case, you would probably feel only a slight or no emotional reaction. But if you believed numbers 2 or 3 to be true, you may be left feeling sad or angry. So how you interpret or understand a situation becomes very important in how you feel or experience emotion. If you believed numbers 1 or 4 to be the case, you may decide when you get home to give the person a call to see how they are. On the other hand, if you believed number 2 or 3 to be true, you may go home and think about why nobody likes you (even though you do not know this to be the case), or you may have an argument with a friend or partner. These are all examples of how our mood or emotion affects how we behave. If you refer to the list of common cognitive errors, you will see that the errors for numbers 2 and 3 could be *jumping to conclusions, mind-reading* or *fortune-telling*. They could also be an example of a *negative mental filter* if you've previously had lots of positive experiences with the person you think is ignoring you. There are no right or wrong answers. A cognitive error or distortion may fall under the heading of more than one category. Indeed, if everything always had to be either right or wrong, then you may have fallen into the trap of *all-or-nothing thinking*, another cognitive error.

Recognising unhelpful thinking

Unhelpful, negative thoughts can often be identified by some of their characteristics. They are often *automatic*; they pop into your head immediately and of their own accord. One negative thought often sets off a chain of others. The thoughts are distorted and/or unhelpful because they help maintain negative moods and may contain one or more cognitive errors as described earlier. They are also *involuntary* and out of your control so you can't just switch them off or stop them. In fact, trying to stop these thoughts has the opposite effect. It tends to make you think about things longer than if you were to pay little or no attention to them and let them pass through. And negative thoughts *appear logical and plausible*.

For all these reasons, we tend to believe in our negative automatic thoughts and may not question their truthfulness. But it is important to remember they are just one possible explanation and there will always be other, alternative ways of looking at things. One of the mottos of CBT is that 'thoughts are not the same as facts', meaning even though our thoughts may be based on some facts, cognitive biases can exaggerate them to make them more like fiction.

This section is specifically designed to help you identify, and deal with, some of the negative thinking that accompanies your DPAFU, as we explain how to complete a Thought Record. As you've worked through the previous sections, you may have kept a diary and/or tried to fit your personal experience of DPAFU into the personal pattern model described. Many of the negative automatic thoughts you have pop into your head without you giving them very much consideration. Research has shown that having negative thoughts can affect your mood. You won't be surprised to learn that thoughts that focus on potential loss of control, loss of your effectiveness as a person and loss of sensations and emotions result in a lowered mood. Thoughts of perceived danger, on the other hand, tend to lead to worry and anxiety.

CBT approaches are based on *measurement*. You can rate or give a numerical value to the strength of your belief that something is true. For example, suppose you were asked how much you believed your eye colour to be blue. Those of you with blue eyes would say 100 per cent true, while those of you with brown or green eyes would say 0 per cent true. That's a straightforward example, but what about things that are not so clear-cut? Imagine you were asked to rate whether a Prime Minister is a good person. This would be difficult to answer with a 0 or 100 per cent. And everyone would be entitled to give their own score – there is no right answer. In much the same way, we can rate how much we believe something to be true; for example, using a scoring system where 0 means 'not in the slightest' through to 10 meaning 'absolutely no doubt'.

Next, we can see how having negative automatic thoughts affects our mood. These thoughts can be very fleeting, so much so that it is sometimes quite hard to slow the process down enough to capture our thoughts. Despite this, the effect on our mood is often profound and long-lasting. Look at an example from Patrick in the table overleaf. The context here was that Patrick had been invited to meet with some friends. He had a negative automatic thought, 'There's no point in going out as I never enjoy it', and this led him to feelings of sadness and hopelessness. He rated his sadness and hopelessness on a scale of 0 per cent (none at all) to 100 per cent (as bad as it could get).

Patrick's Negative Automatic Thought Record

Situation	Negative automatic thought	Mood
My friend invites me to come out with others	There's no point in going out as I never enjoy it.	Sadness 70% Hopelessness 80%

To challenge negative thoughts, we can use a CBT technique called a Thought Record. This is a bit like putting your negative thoughts on trial. You look at the evidence for, and against, these negative thoughts (rather like the evidence that the prosecution and defence lawyers might produce in a courtroom). Believing totally in your negative thoughts, without looking to see if there are any counter-arguments, is like only having a prosecution lawyer in a trial. Just imagine being in court without a defence lawyer – the jury would only hear one side of the story (the accusations against you) and would find you guilty. That's what it's like if you listen to your negative thoughts without trying to defend yourself. Using a Thought Record helps you to examine the evidence from which you derive your negative thoughts. It also helps you to learn how to challenge this evidence with your own counter-evidence. Only once you have listed both the negative and the positive evidence are you able to act as your own judge and jury. This will allow you to come up with a *balanced viewpoint* that considers *all* the evidence. An example of how this counter-evidence can be gathered and recorded is shown in Patrick's Thought Record below.

The next step then for Patrick is to think about the evidence that supports his thought. Our thoughts don't emerge from nowhere. We are likely to have a reason for thinking the way we do. However, we rarely examine the evidence to see how strong or valid it is. Instead, with negative automatic thoughts, we tend to just accept that these are true. To stop believing our negative automatic thoughts, or to believe them less, we need to examine them closely, and not simply accept them. Only when you challenge your thoughts do you gain the power to change them – and by changing your thoughts you can change your moods. Patrick's Thought Record includes an example to give you a better idea of how this works. He states, 'When I went out last Tuesday I felt really ill and went home early.' You can see how his evidence is a bit weak. Only one piece of evidence is used to support the negative automatic thought and it seems like an overgeneralisation.

To start believing your negative thoughts less and to start feeling better about the situation, you must find the best possible counter-evidence, the best 'defence' against your negative thought and your defence needs to win the case. Imagine you were paying a very expensive barrister to speak in your defence – what would you want them to say?

The trial metaphor is useful as, just as in a trial, you should only allow factual evidence to be presented. This helps to prevent any speculation, opinion or feelings being used as evidence for either the prosecution case or the defence case. If you use the same criteria when completing a Thought Record, it reduces the potential for thinking errors. It can take some time to get used to thinking up an argument against your own beliefs, thoughts, ideas and images, but once you've mastered it, the benefits are very significant.

Once you have both sets of evidence – for and against – you can weigh them up, taking into account both sides of the argument. This will help you come up with a balanced or alternative thought that summarises and considers *both* sets of evidence. Continuing the trial metaphor, this is like the judge and jury summing up and producing a verdict. Finally, you need to re-evaluate your original emotions now you have new evidence and a more balanced thought.

Let's have a look at Patrick's example, and we have included a blank Thought Record for you to fill in or copy in Appendix II on page 270:

Patrick's Thought Record

Situation	Negative Automatic Thought (NAT)	Moods 0% to 100%	Evidence for NAT	Evidence against NAT	Balanced thought	Re-rate moods
Sunday evening. Simon called me to invite me to meet up with his friends.	There's no point in going out, I never enjoy it.	Sadness 70% Hopelessness 80%	When I went out last Tuesday, I felt really ill and went home early.	I did go to the cinema last month with Jane and had a good time. Even when I felt ill last month I stayed out and by the end of the night I felt better. I enjoyed 6 out of 10 evenings out. That is more than half of the time.	Although I had a bad time last Tuesday, overall I enjoy myself when I am out.	Sadness 25% Hopelessness 30%

Cognitive behavioural therapy is *not* simply about trying to replace negative views with positive ones. It is about challenging your old views, ideas and beliefs by generating alternative viewpoints and re-evaluating your beliefs in light of the new evidence or your new views.

A word of warning: it can be very difficult to identify negative automatic thoughts when you first start. In treatment with a therapist, people are often given the analogy of learning to read. At first it feels slow and difficult to sound out each of the words. We may also need to use our finger to guide us along. Over time, we become faster and more fluent. In the end, we can spot words at great distances and no longer need our finger to keep our place. Another useful analogy is learning to drive. At first, it feels as if there are so many things to remember: gears, brakes, clutch, mirror, indicators etc. But quite quickly things begin to feel more automatic and/or natural so that you don't have to think so hard about each component. In much the same way, this is true for monitoring your own automatic thoughts. Once you learn how to spot them, you can then begin to challenge them.

Sometimes it is easier to work backwards. If you find yourself feeling an emotion suddenly, out of the blue or very intensely, stop and try to remember what you were just thinking about. Or you may find that certain situations trigger thoughts or feelings. Try to identify these situations and capture the thoughts, ideas and images that accompany them. To start with, just try to recognise or become aware of your thoughts, ideas, beliefs and images. For some people, this is easier to do while relaxing, perhaps sitting quietly or going for a walk. Once you become aware of your thoughts, you need to decide which ones are unhelpful and leave you feeling upset or worried. Then look through the list of common cognitive errors on page 140. Which, if any, are you making? Next, using a Thought Record like the one above, consider how much you believe the thought and think through the evidence you have to believe it. Once you have started to identify your negative thoughts, ideas or beliefs, and any cognitive errors, you can then set about changing them.

One way of doing this is to challenge them. This process is referred to by psychologists as *cognitive restructuring*, and it encourages you to re-evaluate your own thinking. You can do this by acting like a scientist and gathering evidence to support your belief. Once you've done this, you can then begin to generate alternative views. If you get stuck, come back to it when your mood is better. Or ask other people what they would think if they were in a similar situation. Then consider the advantages and disadvantages for each of the ways of thinking. How do these various thoughts, beliefs, ideas and images affect your mood? Are you making cognitive errors? What might be the best way of looking at things?

Have a look at the following example:

I feel that every time I go out socially my DPAFU gets worse so I don't bother to go out now. My workmates used to ask me out all the time but they hardly bother now. I think it's because they don't really like me.

There are several negative thought patterns here. Let's take the first statement: '. . . *every time I go out socially my DPAFU* gets worse . . .' What evidence do you have? *Well, the last time I went out it happened and I think it did the time before that.* Do you have any evidence of when it didn't happen? *Yes, it didn't get worse when I went out for a meal with a friend, and the time I went to the pub straight after work I felt great. The advantage of thinking this way is that if I am ill I won't make a fool of myself by being around other people, and if they don't really like me then I won't be there anyway. But the disadvantages are that I often feel lonely and being in all the time on my own makes me feel depressed. It also means that I tend to dwell on how I feel and why I have this condition.*

I'm making the cognitive error of overgeneralisation. This means that I tend to hang on to negative information and apply it to all situations. What might be an alternative or more balanced thought? *A better way to look at this situation might be to think that sometimes I'm aware of DPAFU sensations, but sometimes I'm not. At least by going out I cheer myself up, don't go over and over things in my head and don't get more depressed.*

The second negative thought is that '*my workmates don't like me*'. What evidence do you have? *Well, they hardly ever ask me to go out with them anymore. Even though I don't really want to go, it does make me feel sad.* Do you have any evidence of when it didn't happen? *Yes, they did ask me to go out two weeks ago for a leaving do, but I said no because I thought I would feel too unwell. The advantages of thinking this way are that if they don't really like me I won't be there, and that they will probably have a better time without me. But the disadvantages are that I often feel lonely and being in all the time on my own makes me feel depressed. And in the past, I have had a few good nights out with them.* What might be an alternative or more balanced thought? *I can see that if every time someone asked me out and I said 'no', very soon they might stop asking. Not because they didn't like me – just because they assumed I didn't want to go out. I can't possibly know that they would have a better time without me because I wouldn't be there to see. If I think this way then I don't feel so bad. The cognitive error I'm making is a mixture of emotional reasoning and jumping to conclusions. I often jump to the conclusion that I will feel worse if I go out, but I do have evidence that is not always the case. In fact, it is the least likely outcome. Just because I feel something is true doesn't mean that it is!*

The main point to note here is that there can be many different explanations for why and how people behave and that we can interpret that behaviour in many ways depending on how we're feeling at the time. The key to challenging negative thinking is to examine all the possible explanations that we (and other people) might be able to come up with to try to get a more balanced viewpoint.

Completing Thought Records

In summary, filling in a Thought Record should include the following steps:

1. In **column 1**, note down the situation when the thought occurred, including when (i.e. day, date or time), where you were, what you were doing (briefly) and who you were with. Try to picture yourself back in the situation as vividly as possible.

2. In **column 2**, identify the actual negative automatic thought (or NAT) as it came to you. Write this out in as much detail as possible, as though you were actually speaking or thinking it. If you had an image, try to put down as much as you are able in words. Don't worry if you find it hard to identify the thought immediately. Just let your mind go back to the situation and gradually the thought will come back to you. This thought is likely to be closely linked to the negative emotions you've listed.

3. In **column 3**, write down all the emotions that you felt at the time. These should be single words such as 'sad', 'angry', 'hopeless', 'frightened', etc. Try to be as specific as possible. For instance, if you felt distressed, try to unpick what individual moods you were experiencing. Rate each mood state from 0 (not at all) to 100 (the worst you have ever felt or the strongest the emotion could ever be for you). So, a score of 50 would mean that you felt the emotion to a moderate or average extent.

4. In **column 4**, start to question the validity of the negative thought. Write down the evidence you're relying on for thinking this way. Why do you believe this thought? Are you making a cognitive error? Try to record as much evidence as you can. Think about the type of evidence that you would need to produce in a court case and avoid making assumptions or mind-reading, which you would be unable to substantiate.

5. In **column 5**, start to generate as much counter-evidence against the negative automatic thought as you possibly can. Take your time on this step; the

more counter-evidence you can find against your negative automatic thought, the better you'll feel. Look back at the list of cognitive errors on page 140. Are you making any of them? Try to identify which ones might apply to your negative automatic thought. Ask yourself the following questions: *What could you argue in your defence? Are there any pieces of counter-evidence that you've overlooked? Has the opposite ever happened? How might you think about this when you're feeling better? What would you say to someone else who was thinking this?* Try to come up with as many alternative viewpoints as you possibly can. Once you've generated as many alternatives as you can on your own, you may wish to ask other people for their opinions.

6. Once you have listed all the evidence for and against your negative automatic thought, read through the lists in columns 4 and 5. Next, think of your *balanced or alternative thought*. Using the metaphor of a legal trial, this is like the judge summing up the evidence for the jury to make their decision. Write this in **column 6**.

7. In **column 7**, go back to the list of negative emotions you experienced during the situation. Copy these from column 3. Holding your new balanced thought in your mind, do these feel less intense? Would you rate them lower now that you have looked at all the counter-evidence? Fill in the new ratings for your emotions.

Here's a completed Thought Record as an example to help you:

Thought Record

1 Situation (when/where/what/with whom)	2 Negative Automatic Thought (NAT) & strength of belief (0–100%)	3 Moods (0–100%)	4 Evidence for NAT	5 Evidence against NAT	6 Balanced thought	7 Re-rate moods
Mon 11 Nov 8pm In my living room Sitting watching TV, on my own	What was the point of trying to get help. I have read the book and my DPAFU is exactly the same.	Sad 80% Angry 50%	I still feel the same I just noticed I am still seeing floaters. I don't feel any more real I don't feel any more connected to my wife.	I have only just started using the book and I have only skim-read a couple of bits. I should go back and take my time. I have only tried out a couple of exercises. The idea of self-help is about self-management and the changes I can make for myself. At least I am watching	Although I've read the book, I still need to complete the exercises and perhaps when I've put these into practice more I'll start to feel better.	Sad 15% Angry 5%

TV – this time last year I didn't even watch it.

It is unrealistic to expect a cure. That was really my goal but it is not achievable in such a short space of time. It may happen in the future but I should not set up false or unachievable goals. I need to think about other ways of monitoring change not based on how I feel emotionally.

I know other people have found CBT helpful for their DPAFU and this book might help me, too.

Be patient with yourself

Please bear in mind that it can be very difficult to come up with alternative and more helpful thoughts when you're feeling low or anxious. You may want to write the thoughts down and come back to them later. You may also want to ask others – perhaps a friend or work colleague – what they would think in the same situation. Or you could carry out a survey to get a wider viewpoint; ask lots of people for their ideas about the situation you encountered to see how they would interpret it. Be alert to the possibility that you're being self-critical or dismissing other points of view because you believe people are only saying things to make you feel better or to keep you happy. This is a cognitive error known as *discounting the positive*.

Like so much else in CBT, you don't have to be perfect at Thought Records. There are no right and wrong answers. It is about you challenging your own thoughts. Don't give up, even if you find the task hard or if you find that you're having the same thoughts time after time. This is completely normal; negative thoughts tend to reappear again and again. After all, that's what keeps the negative cycle going.

Also don't be too concerned if your ratings of negative emotions don't reduce too much; even a slight drop in intensity is progress, and again practising these will help make them more effective for you.

Thought Records are extremely important and they're central to your self-management of DPAFU. By recognising your unhelpful thoughts and the impact they have on your mood and behaviour, you can begin to challenge and generate alternative ways of looking at things. This includes your beliefs, the meaning of your symptoms and experiences and how you respond to these. Like much of this book, it's a subject that you may want to go back and read about several times. You'll also need to practise keeping Thought Records. We all sometimes find ourselves dismissing something as useless because it didn't work immediately. You might want to use the earlier example as a template.

Reducing symptom monitoring

As you learn more about what is happening to you and come to label or call it DPAFU, you will probably develop some specific interpretations or explanations. With any perceived alteration in your state of being, it's usual to pay close attention to how exactly you're feeling. You then begin or continue to monitor carefully the sensations or signs and symptoms associated with the condition. In fact, it is likely that you begin to attribute *all* sensations that you can't make sense of to the condition. It's also probable that you aren't consciously aware of this process, just the result of being intensely aware of your inner state. However, this *increased symptom monitoring* is likely to exacerbate your perception of both the frequency and severity of these sensations and so contribute to the worsening vicious cycle.

This can make you very sensitive to how you're feeling, especially if you also think about how things used to be, and focus on how you imagine things are for other people.

Unsurprisingly, these interpretations can often lead to low mood and increased anxiety or worry. Increased awareness of your thoughts and feelings can result in a negative cycle and deepen the distressing feelings associated with DPAFU.

One of the most common traps that people with DPAFU fall into is constantly monitoring their DPAFU to see if it is getting worse. This is understandable. But regular scanning and monitoring of symptoms is likely to result in several unwanted consequences:

- A negative impact on your mood (such as increasing worry and apprehensiveness)
- A worsening of the negative interpretations you might have for the meaning of your sensations
- A greater sense of feeling disconnected from the outside world

In other words, the more attention you give to your DPAFU, and the more you focus on what is happening inside your body, the more you will increase and maintain your DPAFU.

Research studies support this idea. People who have hypochondriasis, or anxiety about their health, may worry that they may have some serious disease (such as cancer). They then spend lots of time scanning their body for any sensations that they believe could be the first signs of danger. Similarly, people who experience panic attacks commonly monitor their body so that they are prepared if they start to feel panic. Unfortunately, this increased physical monitoring means that you are more likely to notice sensations that are completely harmless. If, instead, your attention was focused on what you were doing, or on your external environment, you wouldn't notice these symptoms. The more we notice these harmless sensations, we more go on to notice them in the future – and the more severe we think they are. This then creates another of those vicious cycles. And although this example is for hypochondriasis, the same applies to monitoring symptoms of DPAFU.

On the other hand, research has found that if someone concentrates hard on something in the external environment, such as trying to solve a difficult puzzle, their attention to their symptoms is massively reduced. They then report their sensations as significantly less problematic. As a result, people often say that their DPAFU is at its best when they get involved in something that takes their mind off how they are feeling.

TRY THIS EXPERIMENT

Pick one of the sensations of DPAFU that you are currently experiencing, or focus on any part of your body (e.g. one of your hands or feet). Shut your eyes for a few minutes and concentrate totally on your sensations. See what you notice. Did the sensations change when you were concentrating on them? Did you notice any new sensations? Did the original sensations increase in intensity?

Now try some mental arithmetic. Starting from the number 200, try subtracting the number 7 repeatedly from the number you obtain, e.g. 193, 186, 179, and so forth until you reach 0. When you stop counting, reflect on your sensations of DPAFU while you were doing the mental arithmetic. Did you notice the sensations as much when you were doing the arithmetic? Or did you find that your mind was so absorbed in concentration that the sensations felt less intense?

One technique that people with DPAFU find useful is an exercise that helps you shift your attention. Rather than focusing inwards on how you are feeling physically, mentally and emotionally, the idea is instead to shift the focus to the outside world. This means paying attention to what is happening around you. It's a particularly useful technique because we know that people with DPAFU spend a lot of time reflecting on how they are feeling. This can include spending time thinking about thoughts and sensations and/ or focusing on how to overcome DPAFU. It's not surprising that if you spend lots of time thinking about yourself, you're paying less attention to the external world. This will magnify the sensation of being detached and cut off.

Imagine that each of us has 100 units in our mind to process everything that occurs. We may use 10 units of these to process peripheral sound and vision. Another 10 units might be used to focus on how we feel. If we find we are hungry or thirsty, we may use 10 units to think about what we are going to cook for dinner that night. This leaves 70 units to focus on the task at hand. Now imagine that out of 100 units we are using 30 or 40 to focus on how we are feeling inside, with a particular focus on how spaced out or detached we feel. We've reduced the number of available processing units down to 30 or 40. Bearing this in mind, it's inevitable that people with DPAFU will frequently report difficulty with attention and concentration.

A psychologist called Adrian Wells developed a specific technique called 'attention training' to help change the focus of our attention. The technique was originally intended to be delivered by a therapist, but the exercise we're presenting here is a shortened version for you to practise on your own. As you sit in a room, try to become aware of three distinct sounds. The first should be immediate and close by within the room. You may have to introduce something such as a ticking clock. The second sound should be just outside the room, perhaps something from another room or outside your house or office. The third sound should be in the far distance, such as the noise of traffic. Make sure you have three distinct sounds and try to focus on each one in turn. Practise becoming aware of each sound. Once you are practised at recognising these different sounds, start to switch your attention between the three.

It may help if you pre-record giving yourself these instructions, in the same way as a therapist would guide you through the exercise. For instance, ask yourself to switch from sounds in the room to the sounds outside, and then to the sounds in the distance. Then back again to sounds outside, to sounds in the room, etc. You don't have to follow any sequence. As you become more familiar with the exercise, try to notice as many sounds as you can at once. You'll find that one sound usually takes precedence over the others. It may be very difficult to divide your attention and listen to the sounds simultaneously.

Practise this exercise for five to ten minutes, twice a day. Continue until you're able to switch your attention rapidly from internal thoughts and feelings to the external sounds and stimuli. Although this technique is not intended to be used in times of distress, it can also work as a distraction technique at these times. At first, however, you should try to do this exercise when you're feeling calm and relatively relaxed. As with the other new skills you're learning, it will take time and practice. As you progress, you may prefer to switch your attention not just to sounds, but to smells or visual cues such as colours. In fact, you can use any stimuli that are outside of your internal world and in the external environment instead. Many people have reported that this technique can help them feel less isolated, detached or cut off from the 'real' world. This is because their attention is now actively focused on the external environment.

Winning against worry and rumination

We're now going to look at worry and rumination associated with DPAFU. Worry tends to focus on anxious thoughts about what might happen in the future, whereas rumination typically is about thinking about events in the past which can't be changed, or about asking yourself questions that can't be answered. Both these types of thinking processes are unhelpful as they don't lead you to find any answers or solutions but instead go round and round, making you feel more anxious or depressed. They are like the processes by which negative automatic thoughts keep going. It's a bit like we become a dog with a bone – the negative automatic thought is like the bone and the worry and rumination is like the chewing. These thoughts can be specific; for example, worrying about what caused the DPAFU in the first place or what the result might be. Or the worries may be more general; for example, worrying about your future or the state of the world. Of course, you might also worry about how much you worry! Whatever your concerns, we hope the following pages will help.

One of the key ways of managing these types of thought processes is to become aware of what exactly it is that you are worried about. What are the thoughts that go round and round in your head? Are they about the same subject? Psychologists call these repetitive, intrusive and unwanted thoughts *ruminations*. People often find themselves going over and over the same worries because they believe that eventually they'll be able to work them through. But going over and over the same thoughts often leaves you feeling as if you're going to drive yourself mad. Worrying can be very unhelpful. Often people worry about things that have happened in the past or dwell on what might have happened if things had been done differently. But, of course, the past can't be changed by worrying about it.

People also worry about how to prevent bad things happening in the future. Sometimes it's helpful to separate out your worries about the past from your anxieties about the future; it's part of trying to be clear about what's behind your feelings of anxiety or uneasiness. Events that have happened in the past can't be changed, as we've said, and going over and over them in your mind often leads to further feelings of anxiety and low mood. Clearly this is not a helpful strategy. Likewise, when we go over all of the things that could possibly happen to us in the future, we often feel increased anxiety and stress. Again, the aim here is to adopt a more balanced viewpoint.

Ask yourself how likely it is that something bad will happen, and be careful that you are not using *emotional reasoning* (one of the cognitive errors) to justify how you feel. Imagine that you believed very strongly that the most likely thing to happen when you left the house that day was that you would be abducted by aliens! It's not likely that many of us would choose to leave the house – no matter how unlikely it was – if we believed this to be 100 per cent true, but how might we behave if we believed it to be 40 per cent true? Well, we might leave the house but remain vigilant. What if we believed it was 1 per cent likely? Then we would probably not give it a second thought. It's important to spend some time identifying the types of worries and anxieties you have as they very often have a significant impact on our behaviour.

It can be very useful to classify your worries into those that are about practical issues that you can do something about, and those that are hypothetical about something that might (or might not) happen in the future. For those where you can take some action, we recommend that you use the problem-solving strategies outlined in the next session. Approaching your worries, rather than avoiding them, will really help.

However, if your worries are hypothetical we suggest that learning to defer your worries to think about at a later point in the day during allocated *worry time* will benefit you. Half an hour per day is usually plenty. Plan this dedicated worry time for a time of day that suits you best; for example, when you return from work, after you've eaten dinner or when the children are in bed. Don't leave it too late in the evening, though, as this may impact on your sleep. Stick to the same time every day. When you find yourself starting to worry, say to yourself that you will deal with this later during your worry time and that thinking about it now will not help. Jot down the worry for later, if this helps you set it aside. Once you have set your worry aside, use an activity that will bring your mind back to the present moment, such as a few moments of mindful awareness. Like all of the other suggestions and exercises in this book, this one will take time and practice to master.

For your first worry session, you'll need a sheet of paper and a pen. A postcard will be enough once you're used to the technique. Make a note of the worry or anxiety that bothers you the most. Then begin to challenge the worry in much the same way as you would in a Thought Record. Imagine what other people might say; look at what evidence you have; are there any alternative ideas, thoughts and beliefs? What can you begin to do to address each worry? Write your responses underneath the worry. Try to fit each worry on to one sheet or card. At the end of the half hour, just stop. You can come back to the worry again the next day. Try to identify and tackle a different worry during each worry time. You'll be surprised at how similar many of the worries are.

SAMPLE WORRY CARD

My DPAFU can't be cured and I'll be like this for ever

I don't know that for a fact. It just feels that way. I'm using emotional reasoning and that is prone to error.

Even if it doesn't go away completely, I can manage it better. Then the impact it has on my life will be minimal.

I've read on a website that it does go away for some people when they stop worrying about it.

Going over and over it in my head is not going to help; if anything, it'll make things worse.

I am going to practise attention training as a way of trying to stop me focusing on my symptoms.

Eventually you'll have a set of worry cards that cover all of the issues that cause you worry or anxiety. This means that when you have a specific or general worry you'll be able to turn to the card and look at what you've written. You may wish to add more each time or remove the things that are no longer applicable. Over time, you'll become more practised in your responses to your worries and will begin to know them off by heart. Then when the worry pops into your head you'll have an automatic response. Gradually, your worries will become fewer as you postpone them until worry time. This will mean you'll be able to deal with them quickly and effectively.

Like many of the exercises in this book, you can ask other people – maybe friends, family or work colleagues – how they might respond to a given worry or anxiety. You can then incorporate their answers into your own to help you generate new ways of thinking. You can also rewrite the cards as your ideas and thoughts change. For example, after reading the section on problem-solving, you may wish to draw up a list of the advantages (benefits) and disadvantages (costs) of having such a worry, or what it means to you if you don't worry.

Resolving Rumination

Rumination is frequently about things we've done in the past or current problems that we can't seem to resolve. Similarly, we might think that this rumination is helping us, so here's something to try to see if it does. Identify and rate your moods out of ten before a period of rumination and then repeat this after ruminating. Do you feel better or worse? Has this helped resolve your problems at all? If you are doing useful thinking, then you should feel better, right? If you feel worse, then it is likely you are ruminating rather than solving your problems. This exercise will motivate you to cut out the rumination as you will see how unhelpful it is to you.

Often, we don't even notice when we've slipped into ruminating, we just notice that time has drifted by. One of the first steps, therefore, is to bring our awareness to when we are ruminating so we can stop it sooner before it affects our mood. Just as we've described above for worry, a key point then is to write down what is going through your mind to capture the exact thoughts. In doing this, you'll probably find that the thoughts are very similar to each other – although it probably doesn't feel like that when they are in your mind. Having them written down allows you to step back from them and gain some distance and perspective, which is a helpful first step. Using a Thought Record can then help you to generate a more helpful alternative balanced thought.

A quick tip for completing Thought Records with worry and rumination thoughts is that these are often in the form of a question, such as 'What if I don't get better?' or 'Why did this happen to me?' It's not possible to put a question on trial and so what you need to do is to change these questions into a statement. Ask yourself what it is that you are really concerned about to get at the root of the problem.

For example, the statement might be 'I won't get better' or 'I caused this to happen to me'. With these statements you will find it easier to look for the evidence for and against to complete the Thought Record.

Another useful strategy for rumination is to get up and do something active. An analogy here is like listening to a stuck record; rather than sitting listening to it going round and round, you need to get up and change it. Distraction is helpful to break the cycle of rumination. The best types of distraction are activities that are either physically or mentally engaging, or both. Get up, get out and get going! In the long term, however, distraction is only a temporary measure as the worries and rumination will tend to come back. A longer-term solution is using some of the CBT strategies we describe here in the book to address some of your problems more thoroughly.

Problem-solving

The ground we cover in this section isn't specific to DPAFU. Instead, we're going to show you an approach that's useful when trying to solve certain types of problems, such as when you encounter a dilemma or when you're unsure of the best option to choose.

Step 1: Clearly define the problem. What are your choices or options? This may involve drawing up a list and writing things down. As in the previous exercises, you will need to be very specific. How will you know when the problem is resolved? How will you measure any change? Possible problem areas include: intimate relationships; family relationships; friendships; employment or study; money and debt; housing; legal matters; substance dependency; physical or mental health; sexual orientation; and bereavement or impending loss. Once you have the problem well-defined, you'll be able to set your goals.

Step 2: Think of as many answers or solutions as possible. At this stage, it doesn't matter how unlikely or impossible these solutions may seem. One of the main reasons that people find it difficult to solve their problems successfully is that they're too dismissive of possible solutions. If you hear yourself starting to say, 'Yes, but . . .', stop! Write your suggestion down anyway. Sometimes, unrealistic solutions help you think more laterally and they can help to generate good solutions. You may also wish to survey the advice and opinions of other people and ask them what they would do in the same situation. Once you have a long list of possible solutions, you need to evaluate each of these in turn. Write out a list of pros and cons for solutions that seem most likely. What are the advantages and disadvantages of one option over another? What are the advantages and disadvantages of *not* choosing one option over another? Although these questions sound remarkably similar, they don't always generate the same responses. For example, imagine that you are thinking about ending a relationship. What would be the advantages and disadvantages of leaving? What would be the advantages and disadvantages of staying?

Step 3: Identify your own resources, skills and abilities, and think about how you've coped in the past. What worked well and what didn't work? Do you use avoidance or unhelpful coping methods like alcohol or drugs? What impact do these methods of coping have on your problems? Who are you able to share your problems with? Do you have friends or family members that you can discuss your problems with? Remember the old adage: *a problem shared is a problem halved.*

Step 4: Once you've written down the most viable options, choose one to try out first. Work out in detail the steps you'll have to take, the order you'll need to take them in and the time frame for each. The better your planning at this stage, the more likely you are to be successful. These steps might include rehearsing in your imagination what you're going to say or do. This will help build your confidence when you think through the likely consequences. You could also roleplay the scene with a friend or family member. If your problem is more to do with time management, you might find an activity diary helpful. For example, if you've fallen behind in your studies or work, plan to add just thirty minutes more each day. By the end of the week, you will have achieved three-and-a-half hours' additional work or study. If, on the other hand, your problem is more one of unhelpful beliefs, you may wish to use a Thought Record. As we discussed earlier, you can then challenge these beliefs. For certain problems, you may also wish to obtain expert advice from organisations such as the Citizens

Advice Bureau, Shelter, Mind, or from a solicitor or local law centre.

Step 5: Carry out the solution. Go ahead and do what you've planned.

Step 6: Evaluate the outcome. This may be in the form of a daily or weekly diary and it'll depend on the goals you identified at the beginning of the problem-solving exercise. For example, you may wish to rate the problem as solved, good progress, some progress or no change. Common causes of difficulty with problem-solving include low self-esteem or lack of self-confidence. Or it may be that the problems selected represent long-standing personal difficulties, such as a long history of very poor or dysfunctional relationships. In these cases, more traditional face-to-face therapy will be needed. If your outcome has not been as good as you'd like, you may want to return to your brainstorming list and choose the next most viable solution. Go through steps 3–6 again with this solution. Evaluate your outcome again. Did this work better?

This six-step approach can be helpful for many types of problem, for example relationship difficulties, including ending intimate partner relationships and falling out with friends or family; whether to leave a job or change roles within employment; study problems such as falling behind with coursework or failing exams; time management; problems bringing up your children; and indeed any other major choices that we face in day-to-day life. Remember, some situations cannot change – you may, for example, have suffered bereavement, lost your job or been diagnosed with cancer. Problem-solving is about saying, 'OK, there are some things I can't change, but I still have lots of options open to me as to what I do next. How can I choose the best option? How can I take the first steps?'

11

Behaving in new ways: tackling your avoidance and safety-seeking behaviours

Earlier we saw how DPAFU sensations can make you behave in certain ways; for instance, by avoiding situations. Another common pattern is that you might adopt behaviours that you feel help you cope in the moment, but which unfortunately might lead in the long term to your problem continuing. These are often referred to as *safety-seeking behaviours*. The reason these are unhelpful is that they often prevent us from discovering that the problem would not have happened anyway. An example might be if someone was to go to a social event but always left after thirty minutes as they believed that their symptoms would get worse after this amount of time. Because of leaving at this point, they would never find out that things would actually be fine for them for the whole evening. In this way, safety-seeking behaviours can undermine our confidence and lead to actions that are unhelpful in the longer term. To break these negative cycles, you will need actively to tackle these behaviours. The way to do this is first to *create a hierarchy* of such behaviours. Then these can be challenged with the use of *behavioural experiments*.

How to create a hierarchy of the behaviours you want to change

Some of the earlier exercises will already have helped you identify the negative behaviours (avoidances and safety-seeking behaviours) that are associated with your DPAFU. For example, look again at Chapter 8 'Keeping a DPAFU diary' where you will have been challenged to think about your behaviours while completing your own diary.

Write a list of all the behaviours you noted about yourself in the following section:

Avoidances

_____

_____

_____

_____

_____

Safety-seeking behaviours

_____

_____

_____

_____

_____

Next, look through your list and rate each behaviour in terms of: (1) how difficult you would find it to do (if it is something you avoid); or (2) how difficult you would find it to *not* do (if it is a safety-seeking behaviour that gives you a sense of comfort). Use the scale of 0–10 given below and write a number next to each behaviour on the list you have created.

0	1	2	3	4	5	6	7	8	9	10
Not difficult at all					Moderately difficult					Very difficult indeed

Now write out the list again on the lines below. But this time re-order the behaviours by placing the behaviour with the highest number at the top, and working down through the list so that the lowest number is at the bottom. This is your personal hierarchy of avoidance and/or safety-seeking behaviours.

Avoidance   **Difficulty rating to do this**

_____

_____

_____

_____

_____

Safety-seeking behaviours   **Difficulty rating to *not* do this**

_____

_____

_____

_____

_____

Example: Mina's hierarchy

Avoidance	Difficulty rating to do this
Driving	10
Spending time around people	8
Looking at reflections of myself	6

Safety-seeking behaviours	Difficulty rating to *not* do this
Pinch myself to see if I can feel	7
Go supermarket shopping very early in the morning when it is quiet	5
Check my eyesight for visual disturbances	4

Finding out about your underlying assumptions

Behavioural experiments are ways of testing out the thoughts, beliefs and assumptions that underlie your avoidances and safety-seeking behaviours. To change the behaviour, you first need to identify the assumptions that cause it. Then you can challenge these assumptions, much in the same way as you did when you used a Thought Record. With Thought

Records you challenged the negative automatic thought just by *thinking* of counter-evidence. However, in a behavioural experiment you need to *actively do something* to challenge your thoughts. First, you set up your assumptions in the form of a prediction. Next, you devise an experiment to test whether what you believe (i.e. your negative assumption) does or doesn't come true in real life.

Let's use the example of Mina. In her hierarchy of avoidances and safety-seeking behaviours, Mina rated driving as 10/10 in terms of difficulty. In other words, she saw driving as the most difficult thing she could do given her DPAFU. But we need to understand *why* driving is so difficult for her. Not everyone will have the same underlying reasons to explain their behaviour, even if the behaviour is the same. One person may avoid driving because they feel they won't be able to see properly. Someone else may avoid driving because they think they will become too anxious. Another person may avoid it because they are convinced they will have an accident. The behaviour (i.e. avoiding driving) is the same, but the beliefs underlying it differ.

To find out what beliefs are causing you to behave in certain ways, choose one of the behaviours you want to change and ask yourself the following questions:

- What do you think might happen if you didn't behave in this way? (*For safety-seeking behaviours*)
- What would be the *worst* thing that could happen if you didn't behave in this way? (*For safety-seeking behaviours*)

- What do you think might happen if you behaved in this way? (*For avoidance behaviours*)
- What do you think would be the *worst* thing that could happen if you behaved in this way? (*For avoidance behaviours*)
- What images come to mind when you picture behaving, or not behaving, in this way?
- What would the worst outcome mean to you?
- What would the worst outcome say about you as a person?
- What would be so bad about that?

Keep repeating the above questions in any order until you reach what you feel is at the root cause of your behaviour. This is called the *downward arrow* technique.

So, for Mina's example of avoiding driving, the exercise might go as follows:

Q. What do you think might happen if you drove?	My DPAFU might get worse ↓
Q. What would be so bad about that?	I can't concentrate ↓
Q. What would be the worst thing that could happen if you did this?	I will crash the car ↓

Q. What images come to mind when you picture yourself doing this?	People injured ↓
Q. What would the worst outcome mean to you?	I'm to blame ↓
Q. What would the worst outcome say about you as a person?	I'm useless

Here's another example, this time using the downward arrow technique with Mina's safety-seeking behaviour of only going to the supermarket very early in the morning when it's quiet:

Q. What do you think might happen if you didn't shop early?	There would be too many people ↓
Q. What would be so bad about that?	I might start to feel more ~~DPAFU~~ ↓
Q. What would be the worst thing that could happen if you did this?	Other people would think I was weird ↓

Q. What images come to mind when you picture yourself doing this?	I see myself looking spaced out with people laughing and pointing at me
	↓
Q. What would the worst outcome say about you as a person?	I'm mad

Once you have identified the core belief underlying your behaviour, it will become very clear as to why you want to avoid something or use a safety-seeking behaviour. To use Mina's example, if you truly believe that you'll have a serious car crash if you drive, that you'll be blamed for the crash and think yourself useless, then it's hardly surprising that you avoid driving. Or if you think other people will laugh at you and think you're mad, naturally you'll want to do as much of your shopping online as you can. However, these beliefs are often our worst fears and not based in reality. Just as negative automatic thoughts can be biased and distorted, so, too, can the underlying assumptions that cause us to behave in certain ways. Unless we test out and challenge these assumptions, we will be stuck in repeated cycles of behaviour that maintain our problems.

Devising behavioural experiments

Using the examples above, Mina's driving prediction would be: 'If I drive the car, I'll have a serious accident.' Her supermarket prediction would be: 'If I go shopping when it's crowded, other people will laugh and point at me.' What experiments do you think Mina could use to test out these predictions? For driving, you might suggest she tries a short drive and sees what happens. Did her prediction of having a crash come true? What about an experiment for Mina's supermarket shopping? Well, it might be that she goes shopping at a busier time of day and sees what happens. Do other people actually laugh and point?

To see if your prediction changes because of the behavioural experiment, you'll need to measure the change. To do this, you need to rate your prediction both before and after the experiment in terms of how much you believe your assumption to be true. This is like the belief ratings you did in the section on Thought Records.

0	10	20	30	40	50	60	70	80	90	100

Don't believe   Moderately   Totally
it at all   convinced   convinced

You might already be able to see a difficulty in setting up behavioural experiments. If you believe something terrible will happen if you do something, or alternatively if you don't do something, you're probably going to be very worried about testing it out. So, it's important to make the behavioural experiment easy enough for you to go ahead and try it out. In the case of driving, you might suggest Mina starts with a very short drive on a quiet bit of road. For the supermarket, you might want her to go at a time when it's likely to be only a little bit busier. Start with relatively easy experiments. Just by doing them you'll build up your confidence. Don't try to do too much at once. Some simple ways you can make things easier for yourself might include:

- Starting with something that is rated low on your hierarchy – you'll find this easier to challenge.
- Trying things for very short periods to begin with, and then gradually increasing the time.
- Testing things out with people who don't know you or, alternatively, who know you well and understand your problems.
- Trying your experiment with the help of a friend, partner or family member before doing it on your own.
- Thinking carefully beforehand about how you can make the experiment a bit easier for yourself.

Here's what you need to do to set up a successful behavioural experiment:

1. Identify your target avoidance or safety-seeking behaviours.
2. Rate each of these in terms of how difficult it would be to do or to stop doing.
3. Build a hierarchy with the most difficult at the top and the easiest at the bottom.
4. Choose something easy to start with.
5. Identify your underlying assumption using the downward arrow technique.
6. Try to be as precise as possible about your belief.
7. Rate how much you believe in your prediction.
8. Devise a behavioural experiment that will test out your prediction.
9. Carry out the experiment!
10. Compare the actual result to the result you predicted. How accurate was your prediction?
11. Re-rate your belief if your prediction did not come true. Modify if necessary.
12. Ask yourself what you have learnt from this experiment.

So you can get an idea of what this might look like in practice, here's an example worksheet for a behavioural experiment, and you'll also find a blank one for you to complete your own experiments in Appendix II on page 272:

Mina's Behaviour Change Worksheet

Target behaviour	Assumption being tested	Belief in assumption %	Experiment	Outcome of experiment	New belief in assumption %
Avoiding driving	If I drive the car, then I will have a serious accident	90%	Drive for 20 minutes along quiet roads with my sister in the car	Nothing happened. My sister told me she thought I was a good driver	70%
Shopping early in the morning when it is quiet	If I go shopping when it is crowded, then other people will laugh and point at me	75%	Go into supermarket at lunchtime and buy a sandwich	Some teenagers were laughing but I don't think it was at me. Most people were too busy to notice me.	50%

You'll see from these examples that Mina's belief in her original assumption was lower after she carried out the behavioural experiments than before. Don't worry if your belief rating doesn't reduce a great deal. To achieve this, you're likely to need to set up several experiments that gradually increase in difficulty. Often, even if an experiment has been successful, you may find that you think of a 'yes, but' type statement that provides an excuse for why it worked out this time. For instance, in the example above, Mina felt that an accident was only prevented because her sister was there and kept talking to her as she drove. She also thought that people didn't laugh at her in the supermarket because it was lunchtime and they were all in a hurry. Can you think of further experiments that she could try to test these beliefs out? Perhaps she would need to drive again without her sister talking to her. Perhaps she could try driving on her own. Perhaps she needs to go to the supermarket in the evening when it might be busy but people wouldn't be in a hurry. Look out for any 'yes, but' thoughts you have that seem to diminish the effectiveness of your own experiment. Set up another experiment to test your new prediction.

12

Other treatment approaches for DPAFU

In this section, we'll look at some other treatment approaches for DPAFU that complement CBT. These include mindfulness, other talking therapy approaches, medication and some other physiological treatments.

Mindfulness

Mindfulness meditation practices are methods that enable us to start to cultivate a present-moment awareness that is without judgement or evaluation. The roots of mindfulness lie in Buddhist meditation but secular adaptations have been devised, initially by Jon Kabat-Zinn, and later others such as John Teasdale. Mindfulness courses are now widely used in health settings for a range of conditions such as depression, anxiety and physical health conditions.

There are clear reasons for predicting that mindfulness will be helpful with DPAFU. For instance, self-reported depersonalisation has been shown to have an inverse relationship with mindfulness. Mindfulness has also been shown

to be helpful for conditions where there is repetitive thinking such as worry (about the future) or rumination (about
the past). Mindfulness also has lots of similarities with the
approach already discussed in this book. As our awareness
of our thoughts increases, this, in turn, allows us to see that
they are not facts but instead mental events that are not
necessarily true.

Mindfulness is not about emptying the mind, nor about
stopping or pushing away our thoughts, bodily sensations
or emotions. Instead, mindfulness is about noticing our
thoughts, sensations and emotions as they arise and choosing
not to elaborate upon or evaluate them. An example would
be simply noticing a sense of emotional numbness as it is,
without evaluating it as a sign of something catastrophic. To
evaluate our experience in such a way is likely to increase our
distress. Similarly, if we spend time going over and over our
experience trying to find answers as to why it happened or
what it means, then this is also likely to make us feel worse.

Mindfulness is also about cultivating an attitude of kindness towards our thoughts, emotions and bodily sensations
as they arise. People are often surprised to learn that they are
in the habit of judging their experiences and sometimes this
judgement can be with a negative tone. For example, Anna
found that when she practised mindfulness she had a strong
habit of judging her emotions and sensations (or absence of
either!) as evidence that something was wrong with her. It
took some time and gentle, patient perseverance to begin
to simply notice this habit of judgement and evaluation and
to choose to drop it for the duration of the practice.

Sometimes, people misunderstand mindfulness and think it is about becoming detached from their sensations, feelings and emotions, and for someone experiencing depersonalisation, they may think, 'I'm already feeling detached . . . why would I want to feel more detached?' But this is a common misunderstanding about mindfulness. Mindfulness is instead about developing an attitude of acceptance towards our experience as it is in this moment. This not to say that our experience will necessarily be pleasant but more that we learn not to make our thoughts, emotions or sensations more painful by evaluating or judging them, trying to push them away or conversely going over them again and again in our mind.

Mindfulness is also quite different to other types of intervention as you do not need to actually do anything and, in fact, the task is simply to become aware of things as they are in this moment. That said, this can sometimes be difficult as we are often used to distracting ourselves from our thoughts, feelings and sensations. It is common that when people first start mindfulness practices they are quite surprised at just how many thoughts they have because ordinarily we are not very aware of these continuous mental events. But, of course, by becoming more aware of these thoughts, we have more opportunity to decide which thoughts to listen to and which to let pass by.

Mindfulness is best learnt by attending a recognised training course of about eight weeks with a qualified teacher. Some local NHS psychology services and/or GP practices offer mindfulness courses and your GP will be able to tell you if there is a course available locally. Some further places offering courses are given in the resources section a little later in this chapter. If you are not able to access one of these courses, then you can initially start to practise daily on your own. The main thing is to start out gently with short sessions – around ten minutes to start with. There are also books and recordings available that will help you develop skills in this area (see the resources section later in this chapter).

Below is a brief exercise on mindfulness that you can try out on your own. Before you start, it can be helpful to remind yourself that mindfulness is about becoming aware of your thoughts, feelings and sensations as they are right now. This means the experience is likely to be different at different times and for different people. There is a strong rationale based on evidence from other clinical conditions that suggests that over time mindfulness may help you develop new ways of being that alleviate the distress associated with DPAFU. But it is important to remember that this doesn't mean that individual mindfulness sessions will be calm, pleasant or peaceful! Sometimes it can be boring, sleep-inducing, agitating and a whole other range of mental states! Although it can be difficult to notice such states without doing something to change them, it can be fruitful to simply become aware of them. This then gives us an opportunity to notice our tendency to evaluate, judge or avoid such states and instead learn to try out a different approach. Mindfulness isn't a quick fix and it requires patience and gentle perseverance. The cultivation of qualities such as self-kindness and curiosity is also very helpful for sustaining a mindfulness practice. But remember it is a practice and it may take time to see any benefits.

MINDFULNESS PRACTICE

- You may choose to use a guided practice (see resources section) or instead you may find it helpful to set an alarm for the duration of the session so that you don't need to check the time. We recommend short practices of around ten minutes to start with.

- Find a posture that is comfortable, not tense, but not so relaxed that you are likely to fall asleep. If in a chair, then ensure that your feet are firmly on the ground. Close your eyes if this is comfortable for you.

- Take a moment to release any unnecessary tension from your body. Relax your shoulders and neck and let go of any tension in your face. Allow yourself to sit upright but relaxed, without any unnecessary strain on the body.

- Gently bring your awareness to the rise and fall of your belly as you breathe. There is no need to change your breathing in any way but, instead, you are simply noticing your breath as it is right here and now. The task is simply to keep your focus on the breath.

- It is very likely that before long your mind will wander. Simply notice that this has happened, and gently return your focus to your breath. You are likely to need to do this again and again during the practice.

- As you do this, remember that there is no need to criticise yourself; simply notice that the mind has wandered and choose to return your awareness to the breath.
- There is no need to push your thoughts away, nor to elaborate upon them. Instead, become aware when a thought has arisen and return your focus to the breath. Again, do not worry or chastise yourself if you find you are no longer focusing on the breath.
- You may also find that you have drifted off and followed a train of thought. This is very common! When this happens, there is again no need to judge yourself or decide that you are doing the exercise wrong. Instead, notice that this has happened and gently bring your awareness back.
- As you do this, start to cultivate a quality of kindness towards all your experience, including the mind that wanders or becomes sleepy, etc.
- Similarly, there is no need to criticise yourself if you find yourself becoming aware of noises outside the room or other external distractions.
- At the end of the mindfulness session, it can be helpful to see if you can continue bringing awareness to subsequent activities in your day.

Questions for your mindfulness practice:

- Am I evaluating my sensations, thoughts or emotions?
- Have I decided that there is something wrong with my experience in this moment?
- Am I being kind to myself, or am I criticising myself and being harsh?
- Am I being patient with myself or can I notice that I am being impatient?
- Do I have any particular expectations about this practice session? If so, can I drop them and instead be curious about this moment?

Mindfulness Resources

Your GP will be able to tell you if they or the local NHS psychology service offer mindfulness courses. The following centres and organisations offer local courses and some have useful resources including recommended books and guided practices on their website:

- **Oxford Mindfulness Centre**: http://oxfordmind fulness.org
- **Breathworks**: http://www.breathworks-mindful ness.org.uk/mindfulness-courses
- **The Centre for Mindfulness Research and Practice**: https://www.bangor.ac.uk/mindfulness/
- **The Mindfulness Association**: https://www.mind fulnessassociation.net/index
- Some local Buddhist centres also offer mindfulness courses.

Other psychological approaches

There are a wide variety of talking therapies and most of them are available on the NHS. They're usually delivered by either clinical psychologists, counselling psychologists, counsellors or nurses trained as therapists. However, if treatment is on the NHS, there'll be a waiting list and this may vary from two weeks to over a year. You will need to see your GP to get a referral to the local psychology, psychotherapy or counselling department. The therapy may take place at an outpatient unit within a local hospital, at your GP's surgery or at a dedicated unit within the community. You may have an idea of the type of therapy you feel would best match your needs. Alternatively, you may have an assessment and the assessing team will advise on what they think would best suit you. The Department of Health produces a booklet entitled *Choosing Talking Therapies?* and it's well worth a read. You can access it from the Department of Health's website (see the 'Further Information' section at the back of this book).

Very briefly, one of the main therapies is *counselling*, which focuses on your problems in the here and now. You will be encouraged to talk about how you feel. The therapist will tend not to tell you what to do, such as suggesting coping strategies, but will instead allow you the space to explore how you feel and the impact this has on your life. Therapy lasts between 6 and 12 sessions and isn't especially intensive. Theoretically, counselling is a person-centred technique, but the counsellor may prefer either a more cognitive behavioural approach (and will use strategies similar to those we've described in this book) or psycho-dynamically orientated therapy, where the emphasis is on exploring early relationships and the effect they have on you now. Counsellors should have undertaken a recognised training course and be registered with an appropriate body (such as the British Association for Counselling and Psychotherapy), to whom they are accountable. This is particularly important if you decide to obtain private counselling because it's legal for anyone to call themselves a counsellor!

It is, however, illegal for someone to call themselves a 'clinical psychologist' without the proper training. It takes three years of full-time training, in addition to an undergraduate degree in psychology, to become a clinical psychologist. Training includes a large research project that's equivalent to a PhD. The Health and Care Professions Council (HCPC) holds a register of people allowed to practise as a clinical psychologist and it also regulates them. However, someone who has completed an undergraduate degree in the subject and has no clinical training may call themselves a psychologist. Again, this is something to be aware of if you look for a therapist privately.

If you see a therapist via the NHS, their employers will have checked out their qualifications. By the way, a 'psychiatrist' is a medically qualified specialist in mental health problems. Some psychiatrists have additional qualifications and experience in various therapies, but all will have a working knowledge of psychological treatments and the use of medication. In the UK, the main qualification is membership of the Royal College of Psychiatrists (MRCPsych).

Other than CBT, the main therapy offered is either *psycho-dynamic* or *psychoanalytic psychotherapy*. Psychotherapy usually involves exploring the connections between your present feelings and behaviours and past events and early relationships in your life. It aims to provide you with a greater understanding of yourself. Some therapists say very little and are more interpretive and analytical, focusing on the underlying meanings of what you say and do, while others are more interactive and supportive. This form of therapy may last from sixteen weeks to several years and may be either one-to-one or in a group. It can be effective for people with long-term difficulties such as relationship problems, low self-esteem and depression. Some people find this form of treatment difficult because you'll be expected to talk about potentially painful past experiences without necessarily being given the tools to help you cope. Instead, you have to self-manage your emotions during the course of the therapy.

There are other forms of therapy that are well-respected but not always routinely available on the NHS, such as *schema therapy, Acceptance and Commitment Therapy (ACT)* and *cognitive analytic therapy* (CAT). Schema therapy was created by a team of people, including Dr Jeffrey Young, who worked directly with Professor Beck. Dr Young believed that although CBT was extremely useful, people who had experienced more adversity, abuse and trauma in their youth needed an approach that emphasised the therapeutic relationship more to allow for a form of 're-parenting'. Schema therapy contains more experiential exercises, using imagery and 'chair work', which allows clients to re-experience and transform past experiences. Schema therapy also has the concept of a 'detached protector' mode, which is like depersonalisation/derealisation, in that it provides a numbing from painful emotions. This is a therapy approach that has a lot of potential to help those with DPAFU and we are now incorporating this form of therapy into our work in our specialist NHS clinic in London.

Acceptance and Commitment Therapy (ACT) combines acceptance and mindfulness strategies with commitment and behaviour change techniques to increase psychological flexibility. The originator, Steven C. Hayes, has used this therapy to help people with a wide range of problems. Some therapists focus exclusively on this therapy, and others will use some of the metaphors and specific interventions in an integrated approach. There is a useful self-help book that describes this approach for those with DPAFU in the reading list in the appendices.

Cognitive Analytic Therapy (CAT) is a form of psychotherapy that blends the principles of CBT and psychoanalysis. It's analytical, but it also uses some of the tools and coping strategies of CBT. You may also come across systemic, humanistic, experiential or interpersonal psychotherapy, and art, drama or music therapy groups may also be available. These are all forms of psychotherapy that may be available to you either privately or on the NHS. Each has a distinct theoretical perspective that guides therapy.

Because so little research has been conducted into the treatment of DPAFU, we're not able to say if any or all of these forms of therapy would be of benefit and so we don't go into detail about them here. Useful books that describe the variety of talking therapies are *Individual Therapy: A Handbook*, edited by Windy Dryden, and *Talk Yourself Better* by Ariane Sherine.

There are some risks associated with all talking therapies. You may well feel worse when you begin to talk about your problems. You may also begin to have difficulties in your relationships as you begin to change as a person. It is not uncommon to experience strong feelings of guilt, shame or anger during therapy, as these may have been previously kept under wraps. This may be particularly true with DPAFU because the main benefit of feeling numb is, of course, that you don't feel anything. If you begin to deal with all the feelings you have protected yourself from for so long, you may very well feel worse before feeling better. But beware of stopping the therapy before you've had a proper chance to see whether it can help you.

Medication

DPAFU involves a change in the state of mind. Because our brain activity provides the basis for our states of mind, experiencing DPAFU is associated with changes in the brain. This isn't to say that there is anything physically wrong with the brain. Indeed, all the evidence suggests that the brain is not physically abnormal in people with DPAFU. However, it seems likely that parts of the brain behave differently when people are experiencing the sensations of DPAFU compared to when they are not. This is probably because of the way different parts of the brain communicate with each other. Communication between parts of the brain involves chemicals called *neurotransmitters*. There are many kinds of neurotransmitter, and medication works by changing the amount, or the activity, of one or more of them. In this way, medication can help treat a range of psychological problems, such as depression or anxiety.

Are there any medications that might be helpful for people with DPAFU?

The first thing to say is that there is currently no well-established drug treatment for DPAFU. At the time of writing, no medication has been specifically licensed (i.e. approved by the regulating authorities) to tackle DPAFU. *It is therefore essential that any drug treatment is undertaken with specialist supervision*. Having said this, there has been some research on possible treatments. A number of medications have been reported as being helpful in individual cases, but it is difficult to know whether these success stories can tell us much about DPAFU in general. For example, in one individual there is no way of knowing whether the person would have improved anyway, with or without the medication. To really know whether a medication is helpful, we need to look at larger studies. A few drugs have been studied for possible beneficial effects in treating DPAFU, including *fluoxetine* (Prozac) and *clomipramine* (Anafranil), but the results have not been particularly encouraging.

Clomipramine is an example of a tricyclic antidepressant, as are *amitriptyline*, *nortriptyline*, *doxepin* and *imipramine*. *Fluoxetine* is an example of a serotonin re-uptake inhibitor (SSRI), as are *citalopram*, *sertraline* and *paroxetine*. There are other drugs called mono-amine oxidase inhibitors (MAOIs), such as *phenelzine*; and serotonin and noradrenaline re-uptake inhibitors (SNRIs), such as *venlafaxine*; and noradrenaline and specific serotonergic antidepressants (NASSAs) like *mirtazapine*.

The main use of all of these classes of drug is to treat depression. Most have been around for many years and all have passed international standards of safety and efficacy. They all need to be prescribed by a qualified doctor. They all have side-effects and certain benefits and drawbacks.

Your doctor may have prescribed one or more of these drugs to you for depression, or a mixture of depression and anxiety, or even to help with sleep problems or physical symptoms like chronic pain. If your doctor feels that one of these conditions underlies your DPAFU then that obviously makes sense. What we can say, however, is that, if you're only experiencing depersonalisation, and if the depersonalisation is relatively severe, these drugs don't always work.

One medication that has shown promising results in treating DPAFU is *lamotrigine* (Lamictal). Lamotrigine works primarily by influencing a neurotransmitter called glutamate. Lamotrigine was originally designed to treat certain kinds of epilepsy, but its use in DPAFU doesn't mean that DPAFU is a form of epilepsy. The idea of using lamotrigine to treat DPAFU came from the discovery that it can prevent the depersonalisation usually caused by ketamine (an anaesthetic drug that's sometimes used illicitly at clubs or raves). This led us to wonder whether lamotrigine might be helpful to people with DPAFU. Early observations were sufficiently encouraging for us to make lamotrigine a regular choice of drug treatment for DPAFU. We now have considerable experience in the use of lamotrigine for DPAFU and have conducted some studies of its effectiveness. Overall, we've found that lamotrigine has a beneficial effect in around 50 per cent of people with DPAFU, when it is combined with an antidepressant medication such as an SSRI or one of the others listed above. These figures suggest that, although lamotrigine isn't a wonder drug, it can have a useful role in treating DPAFU, especially in combination with another medication. However, it should only be prescribed by a specialist, at least initially, that is a psychiatrist who is able to supervise the treatment, make changes and monitor progress as appropriate. We repeat, *lamotrigine is not licensed for the treatment of DPAFU*. When people first start taking lamotrigine, they should begin with a small dose of 25mg per day. This is increased by 25mg every two weeks, so that after two weeks they will start taking 50mg per day, then two weeks after that the dose will rise to 75mg per day, and so on. Once the dose is over 100mg per day, further increases can safely be made in steps of 50mg every two weeks. The maximum dose used in our clinic is around 400mg per day.

The reason for building the dose up gradually like this is that it reduces the risk of side-effects. This is important because lamotrigine can cause a disorder of the blood cells – this happens to about 1 in 2,000 people who take it. To guard against this, the dose is built up slowly and people taking lamotrigine are advised to have blood tests in the early stages of treatment. The tests monitor their blood cell counts and their liver and kidney function. Another possible side-effect of lamotrigine is a skin rash. Occasionally, this may be serious (and is called Stevens–Johnson syndrome), and for this reason anyone taking lamotrigine is advised to stop taking it immediately if a rash develops. Having said that, it should be stressed that the vast majority of people who take lamotrigine do so without experiencing unpleasant side-effects.

In the early stages of treatment, most people feel little or no benefit from the lamotrigine. Usually it's not until the dose reaches 100mg per day that people notice some reduction in their symptoms of DPAFU. The 'right dose' varies between individuals. Most people who benefit significantly from lamotrigine do so at a dose of between 200mg and 400mg per day, but others need a much higher dose. Some people report that the symptoms of DPAFU have completely lifted, while others say that the symptoms are still present, but are less intense and have less of an impact on their lives. When people have a good response to lamotrigine, we advise them to stay on the medication for a year before gradually reducing the dose down to zero. The withdrawal can be done over a period of two or three weeks.

As we've said, some people do not respond to lamotrigine, but at present we have no reliable way of predicting who will respond to it and who won't. However, if lamotrigine doesn't help, there are various other possible drugs. *Clonazepam* (Rivotril, Klonopin) is another epilepsy medication, although it works in a different way to lamotrigine. As well as its role in treating epilepsy, it's useful for controlling anxiety and agitation.

We saw earlier in this book that there's often a relationship between anxiety and DPAFU. Clonazepam can be very effective in reducing anxiety, and some people with DPAFU find that it also decreases their DPAFU symptoms. As with lamotrigine, there is a range of possible doses. Most people take between 0.5mg and 8mg per day, either as a single dose or split between morning and evening doses. Clonazepam can be very helpful, but it's important to know that in some people it can become habit-forming and that coming off it may involve a period of gradual withdrawal by dose reduction. Use of clonazepam should be carefully discussed with your GP or psychiatrist before starting treatment. Once again, we must emphasise that *clonazepam is not licensed for the treatment of DPAFU*.

Another medication that may help with DPAFU is *naltrexone* (Nalorex). Two small studies have shown some evidence of a beneficial effect in DPAFU. However, at the time of writing, information on its effectiveness in treating DPAFU is very limited.

'Major tranquilliser' or 'antipsychotic' medications such as *chlorpromazine*, *olanzapine*, *quetiapine* or *risperidone* are usually used to treat serious mental illnesses such as schizophrenia, and are not recommended for DPAFU. There is currently no theoretical reason for believing they will be helpful, and people with DPAFU who have been prescribed these drugs in the past have usually told us that they brought about a worsening of the symptoms. On the other hand, a few people have found them beneficial. If you've been prescribed one of these drugs, it may be that your problems go beyond simple depersonalisation or derealisation. If you have any concerns, you should discuss them with your doctor. You should certainly not stop any part of your treatment before seeking such advice.

To sum up, various medications can be helpful for DPAFU. To date, the best results we've obtained in our specialist clinic have been with lamotrigine, particularly when it's given in combination with an antidepressant. If lamotrigine doesn't prove helpful, there are alternatives that can be tried. There is no reason why medication cannot be combined with psychological treatment; in fact, it is probably best if it is combined in this way, although some people prefer to undertake one mode of treatment – psychological or pharmacological (drug-based) – without the other.

You should discuss your sensations of DPAFU with your doctor before taking any medication. Remember to tell him or her if you are taking any other medications, as some medications can interact with those discussed here. Also, be sure to mention if you are pregnant or breast-feeding, because some medications should be avoided at these times.

Other physiological treatments

We've been studying some new treatment approaches in the Depersonalisation Disorder clinic at the IoPPN, one of which is *biofeedback*. This is based on the fact that people can learn to control certain bodily functions – such as pulse rate, blood pressure and reactions to emotions – if these measures are fed back to the person, and changes are displayed, in an easily accessible way. For example, if someone can actually hear their heartbeat, they may find that something they do (it doesn't matter what) makes it go up or down. The body then learns what it is that makes a difference, especially if this is rewarded in some way, through a kind of unconscious learning.

Biofeedback training has proved to be valuable in the treatment of a range of clinical conditions such as hypertension (high blood pressure), migraine headache and even epilepsy. We described in Part 1 how our research has shown that DPAFU is characterised by reduced body arousal (arousal is the body gearing itself up for action) and reactions to emotions. We have started to investigate whether increasing body arousal may help relieve some of the symptoms of DPAFU. The person sits in front of a computer screen while electrodes from the skin of their hand convey to the computer skin conductance (arousal) levels. The person can then increase conductance levels and this is displayed in the form of a computer game. The sessions take between 20 and 40 minutes and have to be repeated several times to make a difference. Preliminary results suggest that it may be an effective treatment – at least in the short term. Clinical trials are needed.

Repetitive Transcranial Magnetic Stimulation (rTMS)

One new but so far experimental treatment for depersonal-isation/derealisation is *rTMS*. It has been used up to now in depression and other mental health conditions. It involves having sessions in a lab where magnetic 'paddles' are placed over a particular area of the skull overlying the part of the brain that is the target of the treatment. The operator then turns on a very brief magnetic pulse, which, in turn, induces an electrical change in the brain. The sensation is a bit odd and may be uncomfortable but is not painful. The pulse can be repeated frequently (several times a second) to stimulate the underlying brain region, or infrequently (usually once every second or few seconds) to inhibit it. A session usually lasts around twenty minutes and may be repeated every day for 3–4 weeks or spread out – a few days a week for around 6–8 weeks. At the Institute of Psychiatry, Psychology and Neuroscience we used a single session of rTMS to dampen down the part of the frontal cortex that we think might be responsible for the blunting of emotions that some peo-ple with DPAFU experience. The results were promising. Others have used rTMS to affect the part of the temporal-parietal cortex that might underlie feelings of estrangement from the body (akin to out-of-body experiences). Again, while these studies are intriguing there is not enough evi-dence for us to recommend them as a treatment and it is not available on the NHS.

13

Dealing with problems commonly associated with DPAFU

Sadly, people with DPAFU often have other associated problems. These may have led to the DPAFU, or may be a result of it. As it is likely that these associated problems might be contributing to your DPAFU or be adding further distress, we suggest that you also try to address these problems with the help suggested in this section. More information about where to get more detailed help will be given at the end of each section. We will look at CBT strategies for anxiety, low mood, post-traumatic stress, stress, low self-esteem, alcohol and drug problems and insomnia.

Anxiety and DPAFU

Research has shown that more than half of people who experience panic attacks become depersonalised during their panic attack. In turn, about half of people who experience DPAFU also have panic attacks.

If you experience panic attacks on a regular basis, you might want to get some help that's specifically targeted at that problem. You could use self-help books, or you might visit your GP and ask for a referral for CBT for panic from your local psychology and counselling service. This treatment is very effective and well-established. If you only experience panic rarely or find yourself getting anxious or worried before a specific event or situation, such as a night out with friends, then this section may be of benefit to you. Many of the symptoms or sensations associated with panic are the same as DPAFU. For example, the usual sensations of panic are:

- increased heart rate
- increased breathing
- dry mouth
- feeling dizzy, faint, hot or sweaty
- feeling cut off, detached or light-headed
- distorted vision
- mind racing
- confusion
- thoughts of losing control and going mad
- feeling frightened

Usually with panic, a trigger sets off a chain reaction. The trigger can be a physical sensation, a distressing thought or even the dread of another panic attack. This then leads to the person feeling afraid or anxious or worried. When you feel like this, and you have all of the bodily sensations detailed above, this can lead to thoughts of disaster or a sense that something terrible or sinister is going to happen. These feelings are then taken as further proof that it will definitely happen. Such thoughts usually centre around the fear of losing control, going mad and/or dying:

Increased heart rate	=	'I'm having a heart attack'
Breathlessness	=	'I'm going to suffocate'
Feeling unreal	=	'I'm going mad'
Feeling distant or cut off	=	'I've got brain damage or schizophrenia'

Once this chain reaction begins and thoughts become 'catastrophic', the anxiety continues. This is because of the adrenalin that the body produces. You may feel petrified and your body continues to react as it should under conditions of terror, i.e. increased heart rate and the usual sensations of anxiety. Once again, a vicious cycle is in action.

Just as you did for the Five Systems psychological model we outlined in Chapter 5 on page 51, you'll need to think how your experiences fit this model of the process of anxiety, worry and panic. This will give you a clearer picture of what happens to you during a panic attack. Once you can predict what sensation, thought or image follows on from another, you'll probably feel less frightened. This is because your understanding will grow. You'll need to identify when the panic occurred and what was happening at the time. For example, is there a trigger that is specific to certain places? What were you thinking at the time? It may not be until afterwards that you realise you were thinking about something in particular. Did you become aware of a certain physical sensation, such as a missed heartbeat? (Many people don't know that our heart doesn't beat regularly all day. It often speeds up or slows down for no apparent reason. But this can feel scary). What were you doing? Record these things as soon as possible after each attack while it's still fresh in your mind. Concentrate on the worst sensation. What did you think was going to happen? If you thought you were going to die, go mad or collapse, why didn't it actually happen? What did you do to stop it? Were there things you did or said in your mind to stop the worst-case scenario from happening?

It's likely that over time you will have collected evidence to support the worst-case scenario; i.e. that you are about to lose control, go mad or develop schizophrenia, etc. You may feel that you've had a narrow escape. But how do you account for the fact that the worst hasn't happened so far? Think about this as evidence in itself. What alternative explanations might there be for your sensations? Are there people or places you avoid because you believe that they make things worse? How realistic is that belief? It could be that it's true, or it could simply be that you *think* it's true. As we've already seen, there's a difference!

Try to be aware, too, of the mental images or pictures you have when you feel panicky. These images may be particularly awful and upsetting. If you push them away and don't deal with them at the time, they may make the problem continue. You'd be left with a feeling of something awful, although you may not be sure of what exactly it is.

Panic is similar to DPAFU inasmuch as the more you worry about it, the more likely you are to notice the sensations that you find to be frightening. What are the sensations that really bother you? What do they mean? Do you have evidence to support your beliefs? What might a logical argument against your beliefs be like? You may wish to include in your logical arguments some of these facts about panic:

- During a panic attack, it's virtually impossible to faint because your heart is beating fast and your blood pressure is increased.
- Panic is caused by fear and kept going by adrenalin.
- Adrenalin makes your heart beat faster and your lungs breathe harder. It diverts the blood supply to where you may need it for urgent action (e.g. the muscles) and away from where it's not quite so necessary (e.g. the gut, leading to 'butterflies in the stomach'). In evolutionary terms, this is called the 'fight or flight response'.
- You feel dizzy and faint because you're breathing too hard and exhaling carbon dioxide. This makes the blood vessels to your brain contract, which makes you light-headed.

- The more you worry, the more sensations you notice.
- The more sensations you notice, the more you will worry.
- Noticing sensations appears to confirm your belief that something is wrong. This is the cognitive error of emotional reasoning. Just because you believe or feel something to be true doesn't mean that it is.
- If the worst thing that could happen has not happened by now, that's because it is not going to.
- If you do something that seems to stop the panic from getting out of hand, such as having a sip of water or sitting down, you may end up believing it's the sip of water or the act of sitting down that stopped you from suffocating or collapsing. Again, these are safety behaviours and they may stop you seeing that the worst simply would not have happened even if you hadn't intervened.

Just as you did with the Thought Records, write down your thoughts, ideas, beliefs and images and challenge the evidence you have to support them. Then start generating alternative or more balanced viewpoints. Once again, rate how strongly you believe the thought using the same scale you used before.

We should also mention *anticipatory* anxiety, when you become anxious before anything has happened, and *social* anxiety, when you worry about social situations in which you feel that you may be judged. It may well be that you experience these forms of anxiety in addition to DPAFU. If you recognise these feelings, we suggest you ask your GP for help or investigate self-help. Once again, CBT has a good track record in successfully treating these conditions. There are also some useful self-help books available to help you manage social anxiety.

Low mood and DPAFU

In this section, we look at low mood associated with DPAFU, and not low mood in its own right. If you think you may be experiencing depression, our advice would be to consult your GP and/or a good self-help guide; for example, *Overcoming Depression* by Paul Gilbert (2009) or *Mind Over Mood* by Dennis Greenberger and Christine Padesky (2015). There are numerous others and a quick visit to the self-help section of a bookshop or an Internet search will give you lots of other possibilities.

Like any other chronic condition, DPAFU can get you down and often leads to feelings of hopelessness about the future (we saw this with Alexi's case history, see page 26).

You may wonder whether you'll ever feel well again, which, of course, is likely to lower your mood. Some people also feel helpless because they believe there's very little that can be done to make things better. Low mood doesn't just

216

mean you feel sad; it can affect you on a variety of levels. It can leave you with disturbed sleep, a feeling of exhaustion, irritableness, poor appetite and constant worry. It can make you avoid other people and make you much more prone to cognitive errors (see page 140). People think many of these sensations or symptoms are caused by DPAFU. But low mood and DPAFU aren't one and the same, although there is little doubt that they are related.

Research has shown that we're all sometimes liable to *negative automatic thoughts* and the *cognitive errors* they generally involve. Most of the time, the impact cognitive errors have on our mood, physical reactions and behaviours is minimal. By and large, they do little damage and go unnoticed. But they may become more frequent, prominent and distressing – perhaps following a critical incident, the onset of another condition or as a reaction to an event in our lives. In the negative cycle that follows, the depressed person believes that nothing they do will make them feel better so they no longer bother to try. There is a general feeling of despondency. Hence the old expression that the glass is half empty.

It is these very negative thought-behaviour-mood cycles that people with DPAFU often find themselves caught up in. The way to address low mood is initially to recognise it. Is your mood a cause of DPAFU or a consequence? Are you depressed irrespective of the DPAFU? The first question is very difficult to answer. For some people, low mood will have followed the onset of the DPAFU. You will then need to become aware of the thoughts you have about DPAFU. We know that depression often occurs as a result of perceived loss. Are you grieving for the loss of your old self? Do you feel that you have no control over the sensations of DPAFU and that the situation is hopeless? Do you believe that the DPAFU is a result of, or has caused, irreversible brain damage and that there is nothing you can do about it? All these thoughts and feelings may exaggerate feelings of helplessness. Either way, these are negative thoughts that you can list in a Thought Record (see Chapter 10, page 149). Remember to gather evidence to support or refute your beliefs.

By drawing on CBT models, you can guide your treatment and devise your own self-help programme. You can work to change any one of the five systems outlined earlier in Figure 5.1 on page 51. For instance, you can change:

- how you *think* (through the use of Thought Records)
- how you feel *physically* (you can tackle issues like sleep, diet and exercise or use antidepressant medication)
- change your *environment* (for example, by going away on holiday)
- how you feel *emotionally* (this can be difficult and virtually impossible to control on demand, although making changes to the other systems will help)
- how you *behave* (the easiest thing to change when we are feeling low)

To change your behaviour, start by getting some idea of how your activities are connected to your mood. You can do this by recognising the amount of pleasure and the sense of achievement you get from the activity. To do this, you will need to complete an *activity diary*. This is similar to the hourly diary shown on page 106. Each hour of the day you write down what you were doing (your activity) and how you were feeling (your mood). Next you rate how much pleasure you were getting from your activity and the degree to which you felt any sense of achievement. Rate pleasure and achievement from 0–100 per cent, with 0 meaning none at all and 100 meaning the most possible. Complete the blank version on page 274 to get some idea of where you are at now.

Once you've established your current level or baseline of activity, you can then schedule in more activities that give you a sense of both pleasure and achievement. Have a look at the example below. This will help you complete one yourself for every day of the week. What does the example mean to you? What patterns can you see?

You'll see from this example that there is clearly a link between what we do and our mood. Having lunch with a friend brought the most positive mood, and gave the greatest sense of achievement for that day. Often when you're doing one activity, such as watching television, you may also be going over things in your mind. Be aware of these thoughts and record them in your Thought Record. Again, notice when you're doing things that seem to give you little pleasure. It may be that the situation or activity provokes such anxiety that any sense of pleasure is lost or diminished.

Activity Diary Example

Time	Activity	Mood	Pleasure	Achievement
9–10am	Watching TV, thinking about things	Bored, tearful, anxious	10%	0%
10–11am	Watching TV	Bored	0%	0%
11–12pm	Getting ready to meet a friend	Anxious	30%	50%
12–2pm	Lunch with friend	Cheerful	60%	80%
2–3pm	Sitting at home	Lonely	0%	0%
3–5pm	Reading a book	Angry, unable to concentrate	0%	0%
5–7pm	Asleep	Tired	0%	0%
7–10pm	Watching TV	Bored	10%	0%

Once you've completed your own activity diary (either by creating your own or using the blank template on page 274) for one week, you'll be able to look back over your ratings and ask yourself a series of questions:

- Did my mood change over the week? If so, from what to what?
- Was there a link between the things I did and how I felt?
- What activities give me pleasure and/or a sense of achievement?
- Are there certain days, times or situations that make my mood better or worse?
- Are there themes or patterns that I have only just become aware of?
- What are the sorts of activities I can increase because they make me feel better and decrease because they make me feel worse?

As you begin to address these questions, a plan of action may become clearer. The key to success at this level is to *turn each activity into an experiment.* Don't avoid an activity because you think you won't enjoy it. Invariably, it's the negative thought patterns or the cognitive errors that are making you feel anxious and stopping you from doing something. Complete a Thought Record both *before* you do something and *after* the event. Now compare how you predicted it would go, and how much pleasure and achievement you thought you'd get, with how it went by completing the same ratings. If they're the same, try again but think about the feelings you had before the activity and how they might have influenced the outcome. For example, if you believed that you wouldn't enjoy going to the pub with your friends because your DPAFU would be worse in a confined space and smoky atmosphere, the chances are that you'd be right as you would have paid so much attention to the atmosphere, your feelings of DPAFU and how right you were that you wouldn't enjoy the activity. You'd fail to notice the positive aspects, such as being with your friends. It's also worth reading through the section on managing anxiety. This will help you see whether anticipating events, or ruminating on them, lowers your mood.

It is clear from talking to people who experience DPAFU that they do begin to avoid social situations and being with other people. To start with, this can be in very subtle ways. Eventually though you can end up avoiding other people as much as possible. People often explain that they feel unconnected to, or unreal around, other people. They may also worry that people will think they're somehow odd. Social isolation affects mood in many ways, lowering your mood and reducing your self-esteem and/or self-confidence. Not being around people also confirms your belief that you are 'odd' and that others will see that there is something wrong with you. It also reinforces your disconnectedness from others. Again, these ideas become a negative and circular pattern:

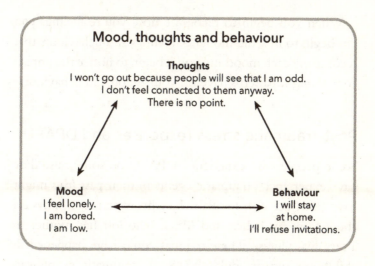

Mood, thoughts and behaviour

Thoughts
I won't go out because people will see that I am odd.
I don't feel connected to them anyway.
There is no point.

Mood
I feel lonely.
I am bored.
I am low.

Behaviour
I will stay
at home.
I'll refuse invitations.

You can apply the same strategies to low mood or depression as you do to your DPAFU. First, identify all the things you believe that DPAFU sensations stop you from doing and the things it makes you do more of. Then think about how much pleasure, stress, distress or satisfaction each one gives you. It may seem obvious that you wouldn't want to repeat the things that made you feel bad, but what about the things you used to enjoy and/or gave you a positive feeling? An example might be going to the cinema. Maybe you've stopped going because it made some of the sensations associated with DPAFU worse. But this may have been at the expense of going out with a good friend on a regular basis. Begin to schedule these activities back into your life gradually. But be careful not to overdo things all at once; this may leave you feeling exhausted or overwhelmed.

When you begin to recognise how you're feeling, you can begin to link the thoughts, feelings and behaviours that accompany each mood and you'll begin to notice the impact your thought patterns have on your mood and behaviour.

Post-traumatic stress responses and DPAFU

Some people who experience DPAFU do so because they have experienced traumatic events in their past (this might have been the case for Patrick, who experienced physical abuse from his father; and Mina, who lost her mother to a terminal illness). These traumas could have happened in childhood and/or adulthood. Some traumatic events can happen at any age, such as being in a life-threatening situation; for example, a natural disaster or road traffic accident, witnessing violence or death, experiencing a physical attack, or suffering a serious illness. Childhood traumas may include emotional, physical or sexual abuse, as well as neglect or bullying.

Not surprisingly, these extremely stressful experiences can lead to significant emotional difficulties in the months or years following. This book isn't specifically targeted at helping you recover from trauma. If you are suffering major impairment to your well-being and ability to function because of such traumas, it's best if you seek professional help, starting with your GP. Again, CBT can be a highly effective treatment. However, there are also some excellent self-help guides, such as *Overcoming Childhood Trauma* by Helen Kennerley and *Overcoming Traumatic Stress* by Claudia

Herbert, which can offer strategies and guidance (see the section on further reading on page 282).

Even if you haven't experienced the kind of trauma described, you may find the following techniques very helpful in combating your DPAFU. Childhood traumas often lead to DPAFU or other types of *dissociative* experiences in which we become detached from reality. Usually this is because a child cannot physically escape from a situation that is frightening or abusive. All too often they are helpless to defend themselves and can only escape using the power of their mind to mentally detach themselves from the situation. For some people this detachment appears to come automatically; for others, it is something that they learn to do over time. Types of dissociation may include having 'out-of-body experiences' (where it feels as though you have left your body but are able to watch what is happening from a distance), self-hypnosis or using imaginary places to which to escape. Experiencing DPAFU can be one of the strategies used to 'cut off' or detach. In adult traumas, too, the same types of dissociative experiences, including DPAFU, can occur at the time of the trauma and afterwards.

If you've experienced trauma in childhood and/or adulthood, and had DPAFU or any other type of dissociation at the time, it's possible that these sensations will recur if you're reminded of your trauma in some way. These reminders don't have to be very precise; sometimes the DPAFU can be set off by the vaguest of triggers, such as a specific smell, a particular word, a place or someone who has a similar appearance to your abuser. Suddenly, you can be overwhelmed with DPAFU. You may even feel as if you are back in the traumatic situation again, almost as though you are reliving the emotions and sensations you felt at the time. Understandably, this is very distressing and frightening

Stress

There's nothing to suggest that people who experience DPAFU feel stress any more than others. If anything, you may even report feeling less stressed, possibly because you feel very little at all. It is often difficult to tease out what people mean when they say they feel stressed. We define stress as '*the feeling of being under pressure, when you feel that the resources you have do not match up to what is required or demanded in any given situation*'. In this section, we discuss stress in general and not specifically in relation to DPAFU.

As ever, the first step is to identify the problem. This task may be made easier by keeping a *stress diary* over a week or two. At the end of each day, rate how stressed you have felt on a scale of, say, 0–10 or 0–100. Be clear about exactly what you're rating. Do you rate stress in terms of its severity during the day, or in terms of how long it lasted? Or do you rate your stress levels in comparison to how you felt, say, three or four weeks ago? In fact, it really doesn't matter how you do it. What's most important is that you decide what you want to measure and be consistent. Once you have your rating, try to identify the factors you feel were responsible for, or contributed to, your stress. Have a look at the example below from Anna for an idea of how you might go about this task, and you can find a blank diary for you to fill in or copy in Appendix II on page 276:

Anna's Stress Diary

Day	Rating 0-100	Factors causing or maintaining stress
Mon	30	Busy at work – things piling up because I was late.
Tue	70	Boss told me he wanted report by end of the day. Worried about it over lunch and found it hard to concentrate.
Wed	45	Took day off sick but I know there will be even more work tomorrow. Worrying about it at home.
Thurs	90	Loads of work to catch up on but I need to leave early to get some shopping. Friends are coming for dinner.
Fri	80	Busy trying to finish work. Dishes at home need washing from last night. All the housework to do.
Sat	10	Little stress since spent day in bed – although worrying a bit about the housework etc.
Sun	35	Worrying about work on Monday – spoiling my day.

Once you've monitored your stress levels over a week or two, you'll be able to identify the major *stressors* (the things that cause you stress) in your life. Of course, you may be more than aware of these already, in which case you won't need to complete the diary. In much the same way as you've done before, the key thing is to produce a well-defined description of the problem from which you can set your goals.

If we look back at Anna's example, she needs to decide if she's finding it hard to keep up with her workload because there's simply too much to do or because she doesn't manage her time well. If the workload is too great, then her goal would be to reduce the load. She could speak to her line manager about what's reasonable and achievable in a working day. If, on the other hand, her stress is a result of poor time management, Anna's goal would be to improve this skill. A third option would be that the stress is a result of a combination of the two factors. It's important to be clear about contributory factors so that each one is managed or dealt with appropriately. There would be little point in Anna's manager reducing her workload if she continued to come in late and leave early to go shopping. While this might feel better in the short term, eventually Anna would find herself feeling stressed again.

Time management means just that – managing your time in a more productive way. Start by examining how you spend your time over the day or the week. You can do this by using a form like the activity diary on page 274. Or better still you can devise your own record of how you spend your day.

Once you've completed this for a few days, you'll be able to identify the times of the day that are particularly busy, and those where you have free time. Next, make a list of all the tasks, activities or chores that you would like to achieve over the day or the week. Remember to keep this list realistic. Take a blank activity diary sheet for each day and plan the day out, scheduling in the things you would like to do. Phase in one or two of these tasks gradually. Just like setting any goal, it'll help if you break it down into manageable chunks.

If you try to take on too much too soon, you may end up not being able to complete all that you'd hoped. You might then use this as evidence that you are a 'failure', rather than the inevitable result of an unrealistic target. Have a look at the example for Anna:

Anna's Activity Diary: 4th June

Time	Activity
1–2pm	Lunch chatting with friends. Late back to work – make it up at end of day
2–3pm	Work
3–4pm	Work
4–5pm	Work
5–6pm	Working late to make up for lost time
6–7pm	Shopping on way home – late for collecting dry cleaning so no clothes for next day

7–8pm	Cooking, eating and washing up
8–9pm	TV
9–10pm	TV
10–11pm	Fell asleep on sofa
11–12am	Ironing clothes – exhausted

Once you have an idea of how you're spending your time, it'll be easier to prioritise those things you *need* to do and those that you *want* to do. You'll then be able to revise how you spend your time. Often, you'll have to balance something pleasurable, like having lunch with friends, with a chore, like going shopping or doing the ironing. But a word of caution – don't use time management as an excuse to avoid certain important activities like socialising!

Here's Anna's list of the tasks she'd like to achieve on a Monday:

- Shopping
- Collect dry cleaning from the weekend
- Go to gym

As you can see from Anna's Revised Activity Diary below, Anna could achieve everything she wanted to with better time management. Giving up part of her lunch hour means she can do the shopping. She can then leave work on time, collect her dry cleaning and get to the gym. This leaves the evening for cooking, eating and relaxing in front of the TV without having to iron at midnight. Other time management tricks include cooking in bulk at the week-end, thus saving time in the week. Think about going to the gym or paying bills in your lunch hour. It's all about being more efficient, rather than doing more or less with your time!

One quick but effective solution to reduce stress is *exercise*. Various research studies have shown a link between increased exercise and decreased stress, anxiety and low mood. Other quick-fix solutions might be to increase dedicated relaxation time, or to talk to a trusted friend or family member. You could also use controlled breathing exercises, such as taking a slow and deep breath in through the nose to a count of two or four and out through the mouth to a count of four or eight. It doesn't matter what number you count to, just so long as the out-breath is for twice the count of the in-breath. The in-breath will energise you, whereas the out-breath is called the breath of relaxation. When you breathe in, try to fill your lungs so that your diaphragm is expanded. When you breathe out, try to expel all the air.

Anna's Revised Activity Diary: 11th June

Time	Activity
1–2pm	Shopping in lunch hour
2–3pm	Work
3–4pm	Work
4–5pm	Work
5–6pm	Picked up dry cleaning
6–7pm	Went to gym
7–8pm	Cooking, eating & washing up
8–9pm	TV
9–10pm	TV
10–11pm	Went to bed

Over the longer term you'll need to challenge your stress-related thoughts in much the same way as we've described for other negative thoughts. What is so bad about stress? What do you think it means? Do you see stress as a sign of weakness and inability to cope? Do you worry that it'll lead to a heart attack? What evidence do you have to support your beliefs? What might be evidence to the contrary? Is there a more balanced or alternative view? Here are some facts that might help with this exercise:

- Stress is part of life! Feeling under stress is common and not an illness.
- Stress can increase the chances of many illnesses occurring, but this is often because of the changes in behaviour that stress provokes. For instance, people tend to smoke or drink more or eat 'comfort' foods that are high in fat or carbohydrates when they're stressed. There is also research to indicate that prolonged exposure to stress increases levels of cortisol (the stress hormone), which can affect and lower the immune system. That's why it's important to recognise and manage your stress as it occurs.
- Stress is not a sign of weakness. Stress affects everyone and anyone. A certain degree of stress is healthy and can, in fact, be helpful. It's what drives and motivates us to get things done. Some stress brings out the best in people and helps to give them the feeling that there are things in life worth striving for. But, like most things in life, it's good in moderation and bad in excess.

The next step is to identify your stress-related thoughts, challenge them and generate alternative viewpoints. Once you have done this, you are part of the way towards managing your stress. The next stage is to develop further coping strategies. The two most obvious are time management (seen earlier in this chapter) and problem-solving (see page 171).

Low self-esteem and self-confidence

Self-esteem and self-confidence are concepts that are often used interchangeably. They simply refer to how you feel about yourself, including your sense of self-worth, your belief in yourself and/or your abilities and the judgements you make about yourself. Improving or being satisfied with these areas of your life can be difficult and may be worth addressing in its own right, especially since problems with self-esteem are often deep-seated and may have been with you since you were young. Again, there's a wide selection of books on this subject, including a few good self-help guides such as Melanie Fennell's *Overcoming Low Self-Esteem* and David Burns' *10 Days to Great Self-Esteem*. We don't look at this issue in any depth, because it's not a major feature associated with DPAFU. However, since some people with DPAFU also have low self-esteem or lack self-confidence and this can have an impact on their DPAFU, we cover how this can be self-managed using the same principles already outlined.

First, as with all psychological difficulties, before you start you need to define the problem clearly. It's not enough to say you have low self-esteem; you need to think how that low self-esteem impacts upon your life. For example, you may feel that you can't speak up at meetings because you'll say the wrong thing or make a fool of yourself. Part of the problem, of course, could be that, because DPAFU makes you feel 'odd', you don't want to draw further attention to yourself. Or it may be that you don't believe in your own abilities or knowledge.

Again, once you've defined the problem, you need to decide how you would like things to be different. This involves thinking about the changes you would like to make. You can then set goals to help you make those changes – and remember that your goals need to follow the SMART rules that we discussed earlier (see page 66). Once you've done this, you can move on to the next part of the process.

Using thought records, try to become aware of your thoughts in the situations you've identified as problematic. You need to examine these thoughts closely and look out for any cognitive errors (see page 140). Again, examine the evidence that supports and refutes your beliefs. Can you think of any alternative explanations for how you're thinking, feeling and behaving?

Another helpful strategy is to carry out surveys among supportive friends and family to see how valid your ideas really are. You could do this by way of a light-hearted game in which you ask them to list your top five qualities or attributes. You might want to predict what they'll say and compare notes afterwards. Everyone who tries this exercise is pleasantly surprised by the responses they receive. An example from Alexi is given below. Alexi described himself as 'quiet, solitary and a bit boring', but his friends and work colleagues saw him very differently as being friendly, thoughtful and reliable. What he saw as negative qualities, they saw in a positive light. If you believe that you possess many negative or neutral qualities, it's easy to see how you can easily end up feeling low or bad about yourself. That's why it's important to challenge your self-perceptions by comparing them with other people's views.

Alexi's Top 5 Qualities/Attributes

Order of priority	Alexi's view of himself	View of Alexi from others
1	Quiet	Friendly
2	Solitary	Thoughtful
3	Pushover	Honest
4	Boring	Reliable
5	Non-confrontational	Trustworthy

Often people talk about self-esteem as though it's just about one thing, and people rate themselves without really thinking about what it means. But usually someone's self-esteem is made up of lots of different qualities. So, another way of trying to increase your self-esteem is to use the *continuum method*. First, give your self-worth a rating from 0–100 per cent, where 0 means that you're not at all a worthwhile person, and 100 means that you're a totally worthwhile person.

Write this rating down so you can refer to it later. Next, list all the factors that you think are important to making a person worthwhile. Try to think of as many qualities as possible, for example:

- Being successful at work
- Having a good relationship
- Being helpful to others
- Having lots of friends

The next step is to put these qualities on to a continuum. A continuum is a sliding scale with extreme points at either end. The ends are the 0 per cent and the 100 per cent points. Let's look at what the extreme points could be for the above qualities:

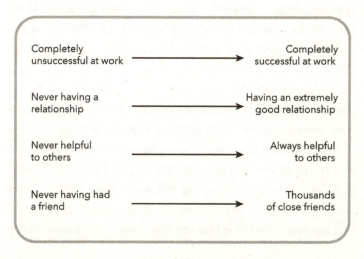

Completely unsuccessful at work	Completely successful at work
Never having a relationship	Having an extremely good relationship
Never helpful to others	Always helpful to others
Never having had a friend	Thousands of close friends

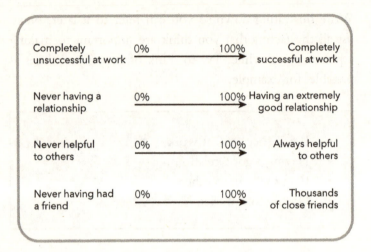

In terms of being successful at work, a score of 0 per cent would mean someone who has never had a job – perhaps someone who has never even had a job interview or indeed any response to a job application. On the other hand, what would being completely successful at work mean? What exactly does this mean for you? Would it be someone at the top of their profession and who has been for a very long time? Who comes to mind when you think of this? Perhaps someone like the US President, or someone who wins a Nobel Prize might be considered in this way? Does it mean someone who has a very high income? If so, how much? Try to think of the extremes and who or what you're basing this on.

For helpfulness, one extreme might be never having helped anyone, never having offered anyone advice, never having loaned or given something to someone, or never having said something that made someone feel better if they were upset. Being 100 per cent helpful might mean that you help anyone who needs it, even if it creates a major problem for you. So, if someone asked you to help them, would you be compelled to do whatever they asked immediately? What would this be like for you?

When you look at these extremes, you'll probably see how unrealistic they are. Can you think of anyone actually demonstrating 100 per cent positive extremes? When you look at the criteria for these positives, what kind of person comes to mind? Maybe a Prime Minister who enjoys the best possible relationship, is as helpful as Mother Teresa and who gets invited to hundreds of parties every night! Does this person exist? *Could* they exist?

Once you've created your continuum for each of the qualities you think are important for self-esteem, think where you'd place yourself on each of them. Consider the different situations you've found yourself in. Are you the same in every situation? Or are there times (either in the present or the past) when you would rate yourself differently? Have there been times or situations when other people may have rated you differently? Think back over your whole life, not just your recent difficulties. Give yourself a percentage rating for each of the qualities. Once you've done this, add up the total and divide by the number of qualities you listed to get your average score. How does this average compare to the rating for self-worth that you wrote down before you started this exercise? You'll probably find that the second rating is much higher. This is because when we think about self-esteem or self-worth we often don't stop to think about the qualities we are including in these concepts. When we do this, and then rate how we match up to the extremes, we often find that we are already much closer to being how we want to be than we think we are.

In the next step, begin to put together a series of positive statements about how you would like to see yourself. Write these sentences or statements on cards or small pieces of paper. Practise reading them out loud. Rate how much you believe each statement to be true. Keep a list of things that you do during the day that are examples of these positive statements; it's your daily self-esteem diary. Here's an example:

Positive belief: I am loveable

Examples of being loveable:

MONDAY

My daughter kissed me when she left for school. My friend rang to invite me out.

TUESDAY

I helped my neighbour by getting her some shopping. I went to work and did a good job. I bought my daughter an ice cream.

WEDNESDAY

I sent a birthday card to a friend.
I listened to my colleague at work when she was upset.
My partner gave me a hug.

Think through all the small things that you've done during the day and jot them down. Regularly re-rate how much you believe the positive statement to be true. As you gather more evidence, you'll start to see your belief increase.

You can also be proactive in increasing your self-esteem. Think about what would have to happen before you'd believe a positive statement more strongly. Or what would have to happen for you not to believe something negative about yourself. Think about ways in which you could test out some of your beliefs and predictions about yourself. Begin to carry out your own experiments to test these beliefs and predictions. While you're carrying out these experiments, draw up a list of treats and rewards for yourself. These don't have to cost lots of money or take up lots of time. Rewards can range from a bar of chocolate, a trip to the local swimming pool or hairdresser's, through to luxury spa weekends and overseas trips. Remember, it's good to treat yourself to whatever makes you feel good, whether that's pampering yourself, going to the gym, shopping or going to a football match. As they say in the advertisement, it's 'because you're worth it'!

If you constantly feel emotionally numb, low self-esteem and/or self-confidence may not be a problem for you. Just as nothing will make you feel good or better about yourself, nothing will make you feel bad or worse. So, while the emotional numbness is a problem, low self-confidence or self-esteem won't be. If, on the other hand, you only feel negative emotions, you may want to go back and look over the section on managing low mood and anxiety.

Insomnia

As we all know, poor sleep can leave you feeling exhausted the next day. In turn, you're more likely to feel 'spaced out' and/or 'disconnected'. You may also find that your ability to concentrate is diminished. These sensations are very similar to DPAFU and you may have noticed that when you're tired your DPAFU seems worse. Poor sleep patterns can lead to negative cycles of behaviour. You wake up feeling tired so you have an afternoon nap; then you find it difficult to go to sleep at night. You lie in bed worrying about not getting to sleep, eventually dropping off in the early hours of the morning, only to get up again feeling tired – and so the problem continues.

Although the use of prescribed sleeping pills can work well in the short term for most people, their effectiveness can diminish very quickly. All too often in the past, the dose was increased and increased until soon people were unable to sleep without taking a pill. Today, GPs are less likely to prescribe them for the longer term because a vast amount of research has shown the risks of dependence with this type of medication. Generally, people are encouraged to seek out more natural methods to improve their sleep. Luckily, there has been a lot of research in this area and there are some very effective techniques available. There are self-help guides, too, that specifically address this problem; for example, *Overcoming Insomnia and Sleep Problems* by Colin Espie.

If you're having problems sleeping, you may find the following suggestions useful. However, you may need to put these into practice over several weeks before you see the benefits. Please don't feel too disheartened if your sleep pattern does not right itself immediately. The key to success is not to give up and to give it at least two to four weeks to reset your sleep pattern. The only long-term remedy for poor sleep is to get into a positive cycle through a process of *sleep hygiene*. Here are some of the golden rules:

- **Don't go to bed until you feel sleepy.** Don't go to bed just because it's 'bedtime' or you're bored. Stay up until you're tired, no matter how late this may be. Prepare yourself for sleep by having a warm bath or reading a relaxing book. Don't do anything remotely stimulating for at least an hour before bed, and don't have any caffeine-laden food or drinks (tea, coffee, chocolate, cola drinks) for at least two hours before bed. Over a few weeks, gradually limit your caffeine intake during the day. Avoid alcohol and nicotine for several hours before bed. Alcohol may make you feel that you can get to sleep quicker, but that sleep is likely to be of poor quality. You'll wake up feeling tired and suffering the side-effects of alcohol!
- **Your bedroom is for sleeping only.** Don't associate the bedroom with anything else. Try not to use your bedroom during the day. Don't lie in bed and watch TV, listen to the radio or

read, no matter how relaxing these things are. It's OK to do these things if you don't have a sleep problem, but when you suffer from insomnia you need to be strict about the activities you do in the bedroom. Instead, do these activities downstairs or in another room to help induce sleepiness. Sex is the only exception. Sex may help you to feel sleepy – especially if it's at night.

- **If you're not asleep within fifteen minutes, get back up.** You don't want to associate your bedroom and your bed with lying awake. When we lie in bed awake, we often find our mind becomes preoccupied with all sorts of thoughts and worries. This can often leave us feeling more anxious, depressed or stressed. So, when you get into bed to sleep, turn out all the lights. If you're not asleep within fifteen minutes, get up again and go somewhere else. Keep warm and do something quiet and not stimulating. This is a good time to try your relaxation, mindfulness or grounding image exercises. Or you could do something very boring instead, such as the ironing or doing a job you've been putting off. Don't drink, eat or smoke (smoking is a mild stimulant). Avoid associating this time with anything meaningful or pleasant. Only go back to bed when you feel sleepy. If you're not asleep within another fifteen-minute period, get up and repeat this sequence – all through the night if you must. It might seem better to just keep lying in bed, rather than getting up every fifteen minutes. However, research shows that the fifteen-minute rule will work if you stick with it – and normally within a few nights.

- **Get up at the same time each morning.** This applies even if you only managed one hour's sleep. Set an alarm and get up when it goes off. It's important to establish a routine. You shouldn't get up later than 9.00am, even if you don't have anything to do that day. Don't make any exceptions – even for the weekend – when you first start.

- **Don't sleep during the day.** Stick to this rule no matter how tired you are. Don't try to catch up on sleep; this will spoil all your hard work. If you find yourself feeling sleepy during the afternoons, go out for a walk, do some housework, or phone a friend instead. Don't go to bed or nap on the sofa. If you need to re-energise yourself during the day, try taking several deep breaths of fresh air.

- **If you sleep too much, gradually bring the time that you usually get up forward by one hour per week.** If, say, you're sleeping until 1.00pm, then in week one set your alarm for 12.00pm, and in week two set it for 11.00am. Do this until you're getting up no later than 9.00am.

A word of warning! Be aware that you may feel worse and more tired when you first use these strategies. But don't give up. Rest assured that it may take a couple of weeks to break many years of poor sleep habits but it is worth persevering.

Drugs and alcohol

Virtually all so-called recreational or illicit drugs have mind-altering properties. After all, that's why people take them. As such, they all have the potential to bring on DPAFU or make it worse. Cannabis (marijuana) may be used by some people because they find it relaxing. However, in our clinical experience cannabis, above all other drugs, and especially the stronger forms (e.g. 'skunk'), is most likely to cause DPAFU. Some people also find that it makes them anxious and paranoid.

The use of drugs and/or alcohol as a coping strategy may be very appealing for some people. In the short term, they can appear useful in blotting out, or numbing, sensations associated with DPAFU. This is especially true when people feel they can't cope with these sensations. But drugs and alcohol are rarely, if ever, a helpful long-term strategy.

On the other hand, many of those experiencing DPAFU avoid drugs and/or alcohol altogether. Some people believe that taking illicit drugs, or drinking excessively, led to the onset of their DPAFU. Others notice that even with one or two alcoholic drinks their symptoms or sensations of DPAFU increase. This can worry some people and lead to them avoiding alcohol at all costs. A few people in our clinic have remarked that it is the hangover stage that is particularly bad if you are prone to depersonalisation.

Abstaining from alcohol shouldn't be viewed as a problem, but it can become an issue. Think back to our discussion of safety-seeking behaviours. How does avoidance of alcohol fit with this? If you find yourself turning down invitations to social events because you no longer drink, ask yourself whether you're using it as an excuse not to go. If you think it may be an issue for you, try re-reading Chapter 11 on avoidance and safety-seeking behaviours.

The usual approach when someone actively avoids a given situation because it increases anxiety is to encourage them to face it. In the case of illicit drug use, this clearly wouldn't be appropriate. We don't advocate illicit activity, and neither do we advocate taking prescription medicine that has not been prescribed for you, nor taking too much of something that has been prescribed.

It's a bit different for alcohol. Drinking isn't a criminal activity and is often a big part of social life. But if used to excess it can be extremely harmful and can have far-reaching consequences. You'll need to exercise judgement when deciding what's right for you. If you find this difficult to do, you may wish to discuss the issue with friends, family or work colleagues. While specific advice on overcoming drink or drug problems is outside the scope of this book, we strongly advise you to seek professional help if you feel you're developing a problem with alcohol or drugs.

14

Managing your own treatment

Hopefully, having reached this part of the book you will be feeling the benefits of what you have read and implemented so far. There may be other strategies you have read about but not yet tried. However, it is not uncommon to feel disappointed that progress is not as quick as you may have wished. Indeed, you may be disappointed that you have not been 'cured'. It is difficult to bear in mind that, for most people, DPAFU is a long-standing condition that may have developed over many years. Because of this, it is not surprising that it takes time to make progress. Change can also sometimes be hard to detect. This is why the use of diaries or record sheets is invaluable.

When you look back, you will often find that change has taken place, but that it has been slow and gradual. Often changes take place on different levels. For example, one man started treatment after many years of being unemployed and living at home with his parents. He always reported that 'nothing had changed, and everything was just the same'. This was despite now having a new girlfriend, doing voluntary work three days per week and living with friends. On the other hand, one woman reported being 'cured', although everything else in her life remained constant. She was still unable to do the same things as before. She just felt better.

If, after working through this book, you still feel that you have not made any progress at all or you have had a setback, you could go along to your GP and ask to be referred to a therapist. This book is not intended to replace traditional treatment. Instead, it is about helping you to better manage aspects of your DPAFU. This is a good point to review your personal DPAFU pattern and to reflect on the different strategies we have covered in the book and how you can best make these work for you, if you haven't already done so.

In Part 1, you will have learnt more about DPAFU and heard about some case studies which may have resonated with your own experiences. In Part 2, you started by setting yourself some personal goals for your recovery. Chapter 7 helped you to understand what may have predisposed you to DPAFU, what may have precipitated the onset of your DPAFU and what currently are the different aspects that are contributing to your present problems. The CBT techniques in the subsequent chapters aim to help you deal with the various aspects you were able to identify as problematic in your personal DPAFU pattern.

Chapter 8 showed you how to identify any fluctuations in your DPAFU through keeping diaries, to see if you could make helpful changes to decrease the worst times and increase the good times.

Chapter 9 described coping strategies that would help you in managing emotional states and bodily sensations.

Chapter 10 covered ways of dealing with unhelpful thoughts, images and thinking processes.

Chapter 11 showed you how to deal with behaviours that may have resulted from your DPAFU and associated problems.

Chapter 12 looked at other treatment approaches that can work alongside CBT.

Chapter 13 focused on helping you with other possible mental health problems that you may have listed in your present problems list.

By using the techniques from these chapters, hopefully you will have been able to address each of the aspects in your Personal DPAFU Pattern in turn. We hope that you have found benefit in this book and are well on the way to managing and recovering from your DPAFU.

Appendix I

The Cambridge Depersonalisation Scale
(Sierra & Berrios, 1996)

NAME: _____ **AGE**: _____

SEX: male / female

(please circle as required)

SCHOOLING: primary / secondary / higher

(e.g. university) (please circle as required)

PLEASE READ INSTRUCTIONS CAREFULLY:

This questionnaire describes strange and 'funny' experiences that normal people may have in their daily life. We are interested in their (a) frequency, i.e. how often you have had these experiences over the last six months; and (b) their approximate duration. For each question, please circle the answers that suit you best. If you are not sure, give your best guess.

1.   Out of the blue, I feel strange, as if I were not real or as if I were cut off from the world.

Frequency	Duration
0=*never*	**In general, it lasts:**
1=*rarely*	1=*few seconds*
2=*often*	2=*few minutes*
3=*very often*	3=*few hours*
4=*all the time*	4=*about a day*
	5=*more than a day*
	6=*more than a week*

2.   What I see looks 'flat' or 'lifeless', as if I were looking at a picture.

Frequency	Duration
0=*never*	**In general, it lasts:**
1=*rarely*	1=*few seconds*
2=*often*	2=*few minutes*
3=*very often*	3=*few hours*
4=*all the time*	4=*about a day*
	5=*more than a day*
	6=*more than a week*

3.   Parts of my body feel as if they didn't belong to me.

Frequency	Duration
0=*never*	**In general, it lasts:**
1=*rarely*	1=*few seconds*
2=*often*	2=*few minutes*
3=*very often*	3=*few hours*
4=*all the time*	4=*about a day*
	5=*more than a day*
	6=*more than a week*

4. I have found myself *not being frightened at all* in situations which normally I would find frightening or distressing.

Frequency	Duration
0=*never*	**In general, it lasts:**
1=*rarely*	1=*few seconds*
2=*often*	2=*few minutes*
3=*very often*	3=*few hours*
4=*all the time*	4=*about a day*
	5=*more than a day*
	6=*more than a week*

5. My favourite activities are no longer enjoyable.

Frequency	Duration
0=*never*	**In general, it lasts:**
1=*rarely*	1=*few seconds*
2=*often*	2=*few minutes*
3=*very often*	3=*few hours*
4=*all the time*	4=*about a day*
	5=*more than a day*
	6=*more than a week*

6. While doing something, I have the feeling of being a 'detached observer' of myself.

Frequency	Duration
0=*never*	**In general, it lasts:**
1=*rarely*	1=*few seconds*
2=*often*	2=*few minutes*
3=*very often*	3=*few hours*
4=*all the time*	4=*about a day*
	5=*more than a day*
	6=*more than a week*

7. The flavour of meals no longer gives me a feeling of pleasure or distaste.

Frequency	Duration
0=*never*	**In general, it lasts:**
1=*rarely*	1=*few seconds*
2=*often*	2=*few minutes*
3=*very often*	3=*few hours*
4=*all the time*	4=*about a day*
	5=*more than a day*
	6=*more than a week*

8. My body feels very light, as if it were floating on air.

Frequency	Duration
0=*never*	**In general, it lasts:**
1=*rarely*	1=*few seconds*
2=*often*	2=*few minutes*
3=*very often*	3=*few hours*
4=*all the time*	4=*about a day*
	5=*more than a day*
	6=*more than a week*

9. When I weep or laugh, I do not seem *to feel* any emotions at all.

Frequency	Duration
0=*never*	**In general, it lasts:**
1=*rarely*	1=*few seconds*
2=*often*	2=*few minutes*
3=*very often*	3=*few hours*
4=*all the time*	4=*about a day*
	5=*more than a day*
	6=*more than a week*

10. I have the feeling of **not having any thoughts at all**, so that when I speak it feels as if my words were being uttered by an 'automaton'.

Frequency
0=*never*
1=*rarely*
2=*often*
3=*very often*
4=*all the time*

Duration
In general, it lasts:
1=*few seconds*
2=*few minutes*
3=*few hours*
4=*about a day*
5=*more than a day*
6=*more than a week*

11. Familiar voices (including my own) sound remote and unreal.

Frequency
0=*never*
1=*rarely*
2=*often*
3=*very often*
4=*all the time*

Duration
In general, it lasts:
1=*few seconds*
2=*few minutes*
3=*few hours*
4=*about a day*
5=*more than a day*
6=*more than a week*

12. I have the feeling that my hands or my feet have become larger or smaller.

Frequency
0=*never*
1=*rarely*
2=*often*
3=*very often*
4=*all the time*

Duration
In general, it lasts:
1=*few seconds*
2=*few minutes*
3=*few hours*
4=*about a day*
5=*more than a day*
6=*more than a week*

13. My surroundings feel detached or unreal, as if there was a veil between me and the outside world.

Frequency	Duration
0=*never*	**In general, it lasts:**
1=*rarely*	1=*few seconds*
2=*often*	2=*few minutes*
3=*very often*	3=*few hours*
4=*all the time*	4=*about a day*
	5=*more than a day*
	6=*more than a week*

14. It seems as if things that I have recently done had taken place a long time ago. For example, anything that I have done this morning feels as if it were done weeks ago.

Frequency	Duration
0=*never*	**In general, it lasts:**
1=*rarely*	1=*few seconds*
2=*often*	2=*few minutes*
3=*very often*	3=*few hours*
4=*all the time*	4=*about a day*
	5=*more than a day*
	6=*more than a week*

15. While fully awake, I have 'visions' in which I can **see** myself outside, as if I were looking at my image in a mirror.

Frequency	Duration
0=*never*	**In general, it lasts:**
1=*rarely*	1=*few seconds*
2=*often*	2=*few minutes*
3=*very often*	3=*few hours*
4=*all the time*	4=*about a day*
	5=*more than a day*
	6=*more than a week*

16. I feel detached from memories of things that have happened to me – as if I had not been involved in them.

Frequency
0=*never*
1=*rarely*
2=*often*
3=*very often*
4=*all the time*

Duration
In general, it lasts:
1=*few seconds*
2=*few minutes*
3=*few hours*
4=*about a day*
5=*more than a day*
6=*more than a week*

17. When in a new situation, it feels as if I have been through it before.

Frequency
0=*never*
1=*rarely*
2=*often*
3=*very often*
4=*all the time*

Duration
In general, it lasts:
1=*few seconds*
2=*few minutes*
3=*few hours*
4=*about a day*
5=*more than a day*
6=*more than a week*

18. Out of the blue, I find myself not feeling any affection towards my family and close friends.

Frequency
0=*never*
1=*rarely*
2=*often*
3=*very often*
4=*all the time*

Duration
In general, it lasts:
1=*few seconds*
2=*few minutes*
3=*few hours*
4=*about a day*
5=*more than a day*
6=*more than a week*

19. Objects around me seem to look smaller or further away.

Frequency
0=*never*
1=*rarely*
2=*often*
3=*very often*
4=*all the time*

Duration
In general, it lasts:
1=*few seconds*
2=*few minutes*
3=*few hours*
4=*about a day*
5=*more than a day*
6=*more than a week*

20. I cannot feel properly the objects that I touch with my hands; it feels *as if it were not me* who was touching them.

Frequency
0=*never*
1=*rarely*
2=*often*
3=*very often*
4=*all the time*

Duration
In general, it lasts:
1=*few seconds*
2=*few minutes*
3=*few hours*
4=*about a day*
5=*more than a day*
6=*more than a week*

21. I do not seem able to picture things in my mind; for example, the face of a close friend or a familiar place.

Frequency
0=*never*
1=*rarely*
2=*often*
3=*very often*
4=*all the time*

Duration
In general, it lasts:
1=*few seconds*
2=*few minutes*
3=*few hours*
4=*about a day*
5=*more than a day*
6=*more than a week*

22. When a part of my body hurts, I feel so detached from the pain that if feels as if it were somebody else's pain.

Frequency
0=*never*
1=*rarely*
2=*often*
3=*very often*
4=*all the time*

Duration
In general, it lasts:
1=*few seconds*
2=*few minutes*
3=*few hours*
4=*about a day*
5=*more than a day*
6=*more than a week*

23. I have the feeling of being outside my body.

Frequency
0=*never*
1=*rarely*
2=*often*
3=*very often*
4=*all the time*

Duration
In general, it lasts:
1=*few seconds*
2=*few minutes*
3=*few hours*
4=*about a day*
5=*more than a day*
6=*more than a week*

24. When I move it doesn't feel as if I were in charge of the movements, so that I feel 'automatic' and mechanical, as if I were a 'robot'.

Frequency
0=*never*
1=*rarely*
2=*often*
3=*very often*
4=*all the time*

Duration
In general, it lasts:
1=*few seconds*
2=*few minutes*
3=*few hours*
4=*about a day*
5=*more than a day*
6=*more than a week*

25. The smell of things no longer gives me a feeling of pleasure or dislike.

Frequency	Duration
	In general, it lasts:
0=*never*	
1=*rarely*	1=*few seconds*
2=*often*	2=*few minutes*
3=*very often*	3=*few hours*
4=*all the time*	4=*about a day*
	5=*more than a day*
	6=*more than a week*

26. I feel so detached from my thoughts that they seem to have a 'life' of their own.

Frequency	Duration
	In general, it lasts:
0=*never*	
1=*rarely*	1=*few seconds*
2=*often*	2=*few minutes*
3=*very often*	3=*few hours*
4=*all the time*	4=*about a day*
	5=*more than a day*
	6=*more than a week*

27. I have to touch myself to make sure that I have a body or a real existence.

Frequency	Duration
	In general, it lasts:
0=*never*	
1=*rarely*	1=*few seconds*
2=*often*	2=*few minutes*
3=*very often*	3=*few hours*
4=*all the time*	4=*about a day*
	5=*more than a day*
	6=*more than a week*

28. **I seem to have lost** some bodily sensations (e.g. of hunger and thirst), so that when I eat or drink, it feels like an automatic routine.

Frequency	Duration
0=*never*	**In general, it lasts:**
1=*rarely*	1=*few seconds*
2=*often*	2=*few minutes*
3=*very often*	3=*few hours*
4=*all the time*	4=*about a day*
	5=*more than a day*
	6=*more than a week*

29. Previously familiar places look unfamiliar, as if I had never seen them before.

Frequency	Duration
0=*never*	**In general, it lasts:**
1=*rarely*	1=*few seconds*
2=*often*	2=*few minutes*
3=*very often*	3=*few hours*
4=*all the time*	4=*about a day*
	5=*more than a day*
	6=*more than a week*

To find out your score, tot up all the circled numbers for both frequency and duration and add together. A total score of 70 or more is associated with a diagnosis of depersonalisation/derealisation disorder.

Source: M. Sierra-Siegert and G. E. Berrios, 'The Cambridge Depersonalisation Scale: a new instrument for the measurement of depersonalisation', *Psychiatry Research*, 93 (2), pp. 153–64. Copyright Elsevier, 6 March 2000.

Appendix II
Blank worksheets

On the following pages you'll find a series of blank work-sheets for the exercises described in Part 2.

My Personal DPAFU Pattern

Predisposing factors

....

....

....

↓

Precipitating factors

....

....

....

↙   ↘

Thoughts/Images   **Thought processes**

....

....

....   **Present problems**   ....

....

                ↖   ....   ↗

Behaviours   ....   **Emotions**

....   ↕   ....

....

....   **Bodily sensations**   ....

....

                    ....

                    ....

                    ....

Protective factors

....

....

....

Hourly DPAFU Diary

Rate your DPAFU every hour using the scale below:

0 1 2 3 4 5 6 7 8 9 10

No DPAFU at all — Moderately DPAFU — Worst DPAFU

Time	Monday	Tuesday	Wednesday	Thursday	Friday	Saturday	Sunday
6–7am							
7–8am							
8–9am							
9–10am							
10–11am							
11–12pm							
12–1pm							

1–2pm	2–3pm	3–4pm	4–5pm	5–6pm	6–7pm	7–8pm	8–9pm	9–10pm	10–11pm	11–12pm	12–1am

Analysing Possible Reasons for
Fluctuating DPAFU Severity

Times when my DPAFU symptoms are at their worst			
DPAFU rating	What I was doing	Possible reasons why	What could I do to change or modify this?

Times when my DPAFU symptoms are at their best			
DPAFU rating	What I was doing	Possible reasons why	What can I learn from this?

Diary for Intermittent DPAFU

Situation	Thought(s)	Emotion	Behaviours	Sensations

Thought Record

1 Situation (when/ where/ what/ with whom)	2 Negative Automatic Thought (NAT) & strength of belief (0–100%)	3 Moods (0–100%)	4 Evidence for NAT	5 Evidence against NAT	6 Balanced thought	7 Re-rate moods

Behaviour Change Worksheet

Target behaviour	Assumption being tested	Belief in assumption %	Experiment	Outcome of experiment	New belief in assumption %

Activity Diary

Time	Activity	Mood	Pleasure	Achievement
6–7am				
7–8am				
8–9am				
9–10am				
10–11am				
11–12am				
12–1pm				
1–2pm				
2–3pm				

3–4pm	4–5pm	5–6pm	6–7pm	7–8pm	8–9pm	9–10pm	10–11pm	11–12am

Stress Diary

Day	Rating 0–100	Factors causing or maintaining stress
Mon		
Tue		
Wed		
Thurs		
Fri		
Sat		
Sun		

Glossary

anxiety: a mood state, which can be brief or prolonged and characterised by negative feelings such as apprehension, dread, uneasiness and distress. Anxiety is related to fear but, unlike fear, a specific object, person or event does not always induce it.

attribution: a statement or belief that something causes something else to happen, or explains it.

avoidance: the tendency not to do something, or keep away from something that we believe is likely to result in a negative outcome. For example, we may not take an exam because we believe that the most likely outcome is failure, or we may avoid leaving the house because we fear that we would not be able to cope.

cognitive errors/distortions: these are common errors of thinking (or imagining) that happen automatically (*see* **NATs**). Examples of cognitive errors/distortions are 'jumping to conclusions' or 'believing that we know what others are thinking'. Although everyone makes these types of errors, they become more frequent and distorted when we experience negative emotional states.

delusion: a false belief that is maintained to the contrary of the available information and data, and despite what almost everyone with the same background argues. An example of a delusion would be the belief that intelligence forces are spying on you from outer space, or that you have supernatural powers.

depersonalisation: the feeling of loss of the self or any aspect of the self and/or of one's identity.

depressive illness/depression: a state characterised by low mood that persists and is of such a severity that it interferes with day-to-day life. It is likely to be deemed to merit medical or psychological treatment.

derealisation: an alteration in the perception of the environment and/or disconnection from it, such that it feels changed, altered or unreal.

dissociation/dissociative experiences: experiences that cover a range of sensations of feeling disconnected from oneself, others or the world. These can include the feeling of being outside, or separated from, your own body, personality, or functions, or forgetting who you are or what you have been doing over a period of time.

emotional reasoning: the belief that something is 'true' or 'real' because it feels emotionally as if that were the case. For example, believing that you are a complete failure just because you feel a sense of failure at the present moment.

hallucination: an experience of false perception that occurs when a person is wide awake. The experience is believed to be real but lacks the physical stimulus. Some common examples are hearing voices that are not present (*auditory hallucination*) or likewise seeing objects that are not present (*visual hallucination*). Any of the senses may be involved, including smell, taste or touch.

low mood: a relatively short-lived mood state characterised by negative feelings such as sadness, depression, despondency, pessimism, self-doubt and/or hopelessness.

negative automatic thoughts (NATs): thoughts by their very nature are automatic in that they 'pop' into our head without control or volition. Negative automatic thoughts are distressing and tend to be linked to negative beliefs about ourselves, the world and/or others. These types of thought are likely to be biased in nature (*see* **cognitive errors/distortions**).

neurological: relating to the structure and function of the nervous system, which encompasses the brain, spinal cord and peripheral nerves.

obsessive compulsive disorder (OCD): is a clinical condition. Obsessions are annoying thoughts or images that repeatedly enter the mind. Compulsions are useless behaviours – actions that you feel you have to do but find difficult to resist. They therefore tend to be repeated again and again.

phobia: a state of anxiety induced by a specific situation, object or event.

psychosis: a generic term, often used by psychiatrists and psychologists to describe a range of conditions that are characterised by a combination of delusions, hallucinations, disorganised speech, unpredictable and/or disturbed behaviour and mood. Examples of these conditions are schizophrenia and bipolar disorder.

recurrent DPAFU (depersonalisation and/or feelings of unreality): feelings of depersonalisation and/or derealisation that continue to recur. Each episode may last for a substantial period of time.

rumination: dwelling upon thoughts, ideas, beliefs and/or images. This process is usually unwanted and/or intrusive and cannot be controlled or stopped at will.

safety-seeking behaviour: any behaviour that we adopt because we believe it is likely to prevent harm and/or something bad happening. Safety-seeking behaviours can be 'overt' and clearly observable by others, or 'covert', which means they only involve our thoughts. An example of an overt safety-seeking behaviour might be taking sips of water because we believe it will prevent fainting. A covert safety-seeking behaviour might be repeating specific words or counting to try to prevent something bad from happening. It is important to recognise that the safety-seeking behaviours themselves do not prevent harm from happening despite the belief that they do.

social anxiety/phobia: feelings of anxiety when placed in a 'social' or 'public' situation fed by the belief that one is likely to be judged negatively by others. A common example of this is a fear of embarrassing yourself while making a speech or giving a presentation.

transient DPAFU (depersonalisation and/or feelings of unreality): feelings of depersonalisation and/or derealisation that come and go, and only last a very brief time.

Further information

Books

Related to DPAFU

Depersonalisation: A New Look at a Neglected Syndrome by Mauricio Sierra, Cambridge University Press (2012)

Feeling Unreal: Depersonalisation Disorder and the Loss of the Self by D. Simeon and J. Abugel, Oxford University Press (2006)

Stranger to My Self: Inside Depersonalisation: the Hidden Epidemic by Jeffrey Abugel, Johns Road Publishing (2011)

Overcoming Depersonalisation Disorder: A Mindfulness and Acceptance Guide to Conquering Feelings of Numbness and Unreality by Fugen Neziroglu and Katherine Donnelly, New Harbinger (2010)

Other relevant books in the 'Overcoming . . .' series

Overcoming Anxiety by H. Kennerley, Robinson (2014)

Overcoming Childhood Trauma by H. Kennerley, Robinson (2000)

Overcoming Panic by V. Manicavasagar and D. Silove, Robinson (2017)

Overcoming Depression by P. Gilbert, Robinson (2009)

Overcoming Insomnia and Sleep Problems by C. Espie, Robinson (2006)

Overcoming Low Self-Esteem by M. Fennell, Robinson (2016)

Overcoming Traumatic Stress by C. Herbert, Robinson (2017)

Other relevant books

Cognitive Therapy of Anxiety Disorders: A Practice Manual and Conceptual Guide by A. Wells, Wiley (1997)

Full Catastrophe Living by J. Kabat-Zinn, Piatkus (2013)

Handbook of Individual Therapy (6th Edition) by W. Dryden, Sage Publications (2013)

Mind over Mood, Second Edition: Change How You Feel by Changing the Way You Think by D. A. Greenberger and C. A. Padesky, Guildford Press (2015)

10 Days to Great Self-Esteem by D. Burns, Vermilion (2000)

Academic articles

Although many of these articles are intended for academics and scientists, they may be of interest to some people with DPAFU. In addition, if you are seeing a healthcare professional, they may wish to track down some of the articles for themselves.

'A case series of 223 patients with depersonalisation-derealisation syndrome', by M. Michal, J. Adler, J. Wiltink, et al. *BMC Psychiatry*, 2016, Volume 16:203. DOI 10.1186/ s12888-016-0908-4.

This paper from Germany describes a large group of patients with DP/DR and compares them to patients with depression. It mostly confirms what Dawn Baker and Daphne Simeon and colleagues found in the UK and US respectively. The link with anxiety and depression is shown while a link to past trauma does not emerge.

'Attributions, appraisals and attention for symptoms in depersonalisation disorder', by Hunter, E. C. M; Salkovskis, P. M. & David, A. S. (2014), *Behaviour Research and Therapy*, 53, 20–29.

The research tests the CBT model of DPAFU.

'Autonomic response in depersonalisation disorder' by M. Sierra, C. Senior, J. Dalton, M. McDonough, A. Bond,

M. L. Phillips, A. M. O'Dwyer and A. S. David in *Archives of General Psychiatry*, 2002, Volume 59, issue 9, pp. 833–8.

This study measured skin conductance (a measure of emotional activation in the body) in response to disturbing pictures and found that people with DPAFU showed reduced responses indicative of 'emotional numbing'.

'Autonomic response in the perception of disgust and happiness in depersonalisation disorder' by M. Sierra, C. Senior, M. L. Phillips and A. S. David in *Psychiatry Research*, 2006, Volume 145, pp. 225–31.

This study measured skin conductance (a measure of how the body reacts to emotions) in response to faces expressing happiness and disgust and found that people with DPAFU showed lowered responses to disgusted faces only. This is indicative of emotional numbing to unpleasant and threatening stimuli.

'The Cambridge Depersonalisation Scale. A new instrument for the measurement of depersonalisation' by M. Sierra-Siegert and G. Berrios in *Psychiatry Research*, 2000, Volume 93, pp. 153–64.

Introducing the Cambridge Depersonalisation Scale – a self-report measure of DPAFU (see Appendix I).

'Chronic Depersonalisation following illicit drug use: Review of Forty Cases' by N. Medford, D. Baker,

E. Hunter, M. Sierra, E. J. Lawrence, M. L. Phillips and A. S. David in *Addiction*, 2003, Volume 98, issue 12, pp. 1731–36.

This study suggests that the nature of drug-induced DPAFU is not on the whole different from DPAFU that is not drug-induced.

'Cognitive Behaviour Therapy for Depersonalisation Disorder: An Open Study' by E. Hunter, D. Baker, M. Phillips, M. Sierra and A. S. David in *Behaviour Research and Therapy*, 2005, Volume 43, issue 9, pp. 1121–30.

This small-scale study explored the use of CBT for symptoms of DPAFU. The initial results suggest that a CBT approach to DPAFU may be effective, but further trials with larger sample sizes and more rigorous research methodology are needed to determine how useful it is.

'Depersonalisation and Derealisation: Assessment and Management', by Hunter, E. C. M., Charlton, J & David, A. S., *BMJ*, 356:j745 doi: 10.1136/bmj.j745 (Published 23 March 2017)

This is a brief article aimed at general practitioners and clinicians that summarises the main symptoms and research, as well as offering guidance for treatment.

'Depersonalisation Disorder' by M. L. Phillips, E. Hunter, D. Baker, N. Medford, M. Sierra and A. S. David in *Current*

Medical Literature – Psychiatry, 2005, Volume 16, issue 1, pp. 1–5.

A brief overview of the clinical features and prevalence of DPAFU, along with a review of the latest in drug and CBT treatments.

'Depersonalisation Disorder: A Cognitive–Behavioural Conceptualisation' by E. Hunter, M. Phillips, T. Chalder, M. Sierra and A. S. David in *Behavioural Research & Therapy*, 2003, Volume 41, issue 12, pp. 1451–67.

This paper presents a cognitive behavioural model of DPAFU.

'Depersonalisation Disorder: A Contemporary Overview' by D. Simeon in *CNS Drugs*, 2004, Volume 18, issue 6, pp. 343–54.

A review paper explaining the clinical manifestations, prevalence and potential treatment options.

'Depersonalisation Disorder: clinical features of 204 cases' by D. Baker, E. Hunter, E. J. Lawrence, N. Medford, M. Patel, C. Senior, M. Sierra, M. V. Lambert, M. L. Phillips and A. S. David in *British Journal of Psychiatry*, 2003, Volume 182, pp. 428–33.

This paper presents an overview of the clinical features of DPAFU drawn from responses to a questionnaire given to patients referred to our unit at the IoPPN.

'Depersonalisation Disorder: Thinking without Feeling' by M. L. Phillips, N. Medford, C. Senior, E. T. Bullmore, J. Suckling, M. J. Brammer, C. Andrew, M. Sierra, S. C. R. Williams and A. S. David in *Psychiatry Research: Neuroimaging*, 2001, Volume 108, pp. 145–160.

One of the earliest fMRI (a type of brain scan that shows which areas are activated) studies of DPAFU, which showed underactivity in key emotion-processing brain regions.

'Depersonalisation research at the Maudsley Hospital' by C. Senior, E. Hunter, M. V. Lambert, N. C. Medford, M. Sierra, M. L. Phillips and A. S. David in *The Psychologist*, 2001, Volume 14, issue 3, pp. 128–32.

A non-specialist article reviewing the work of our unit at the IoPPN.

'Development, reliability, and validity of a dissociation scale' by E. M. Bernstein and F. W. Putnam in *Journal of Nervous & Mental Disease*, 1986, Volume 174, pp. 727–35.

Describes and presents the Dissociative Experiences Scale.

'Emotional memory in depersonalisation disorder: a functional MRI study' by N. Medford, B. Brierley, M. Brammer, E. T. Bullmore, A. S. David and M. L. Phillips in *Psychiatry Research: Neuroimaging*, 2006, Volume 148, pp. 93–102.

This study explored our memory for emotional words and found that people who report DPAFU showed different brain activity to people who didn't when asked to remember previously read emotional words, or words within emotionally charged sentences.

'The epidemiology of depersonalisation and derealisation: a systematic review' by E. Hunter, M. Sierra and A. S. David in *Social Psychiatry & Psychiatric Epidemiology*, 2004, Volume 39, issue 1, pp. 9–18.

Surveys demonstrate that short-lasting symptoms of DPAFU in the general population are common. In addition, DPAFU appears to be common in normal and psychiatric populations.

'Feeling unreal: a depersonalisation disorder update of 117 cases' by D. Simeon, M. Knutelska, D. Nelson and O. Guralnik in *Journal of Clinical Psychiatry*, 2003, Volume 64, issue 9, pp. 990–7.

A report on the clinical characteristics and prevalence of DPAFU.

'Fluoxetine therapy in depersonalisation disorder: Randomised controlled trial' by D. Simeon, O. Guralnik, J. Schmeidler and M. Knutelska in *British Journal of Psychiatry*, 2004, Volume 185, issue 1, pp. 31–6.

Fifty-four participants were randomly given either fluoxetine or a placebo in a double-blind trial (during the trial neither patients nor researchers knew who was taking real medication and who was taking a placebo). Fluoxetine was not effective in treating DPAFU.

'Lamotrigine as an add-on treatment for depersonalisation disorder: a retrospective study of 32 cases' by M. Sierra, D. Baker, N. Medford, E. Lawrence, M. Patel, M. L. Phillips and A. S. David in *Clinical Neuropharmacology*, 2006, Volume 29, issue 5, pp. 253–8.

The results of this small trial suggest that a significant number of patients with DPAFU may respond to lamotrigine when combined with antidepressant medication. The results are sufficiently positive to prompt a larger controlled evaluation of lamotrigine as an 'add-on' treatment in DPAFU.

'Neuroplasticity: Changes in grey matter induced by training' by B. Draganski, C. Gaser, V. Busch, G. Schuierer, U. Bogdahn and A. May in *Nature*, 2004, Volume 427, pp. 311–12.

This brain imaging study of twelve healthy volunteers showed that the structure of the brain can change as a result of a person's behaviour, in this case learning to juggle.

'Prevalence and childhood antecedents of depersonalisation syndrome in a UK birth cohort', *Social Psychiatry and Psychiatric Epidemiology*, Lee, W. E., Kwok, C. H. T., Hunter, E. C. M., Richards, M. & David, A. S. (2012), 47 (2), 253–261.

This is a study showing that anxiety in childhood is correlated with DPAFU in adult life.

'Understanding and treating depersonalisation disorder' in *Cognitive Behavioural Approaches to the Understanding and Treatment of Dissociation*, Hunter, E. C. M. (2013), Kennerley, H., Kennedy, F & Pearson, D (Eds.) Routledge Press.

This is a book about CBT approaches to a range of dissociative disorders and includes a chapter on DPAFU.

'Understanding and treating depersonalisation disorder' by N. Medford, M. Sierra, D. Baker and A. S. David in *Advances in Psychiatric Treatment*, 2005, Volume 11, pp. 92–100.

A review paper introducing DPAFU and discussing various treatment options.

'Ventrolateral prefrontal cortex repetitive transcranial magnetic stimulation in the treatment of depersonalisation disorder: A consecutive case series' by E. L. Jay, S. Nestler, M. Sierra, J. McLelland, M. Kekic, A. S. David in *Psychiatry Research*, 2016, Volume 240, pp 118–122.

A very small study of rTMS given as a potential treatment. It produced some improvements in four out of seven patients.

Classic historical books and articles

'Depersonalisation: a conceptual history' by M. Sierra and G. E. Berrios in *History of Psychiatry*, 1997, Volume 8, pp. 213–29.

Reviews classic and modern writings.

'Depersonalisation – I. aetiology and phenomenology; II. clinical syndromes' by B. Ackner in *Journal of Mental Science*, 1954, Volume 100, issue 1, pp. 838–53, (II) pp. 854–72.

Medical Psychology by P. Schilder, John Wiley & Sons (1953).

'On depersonalisation' by W. W. Mayer-Gross in *British Journal of Medical Psychology*, 1935, Volume 15, pp. 103–22.

'The depersonalisation syndrome' by H. J. Shorvon in *Proceedings of the Royal Society of Medicine*, 1946, Volume 39, pp. 779–92.

'Un cas de depersonnalisation (by L. Dugas)' by M. Sierra and G. Berrios in *History of Psychiatry* (Introduction and translation), 1996, Volume 7, pp. 451–61.

Websites

Website links related to depersonalisation

There is a UK charity specifically for depersonalisation and derealisation, which has useful resources:
http://www.unrealuk.org/

The London NHS clinic based at the Maudsley Hospital:
http://www.national.slam.nhs.uk/services/adult-services/depersonalisation/

A short 12-minute film about what the London NHS service offers:
https://www.youtube.com/watch?v=o7Dr8jt_Ixg

A 30-minute film about recovery from depersonalisation/derealisation through CBT:
https://youtu.be/GWyidaGteGg

The DPAFU Research Unit at the Institute of Psychiatry, Psychology and Neuroscience:
https://www.kcl.ac.uk/ioppn/depts/ps/research/neurobiologialmechanisms/depersonalisationresearchunit.aspx

Other Websites

The Centre for Mindfulness Research and Practice (CMRP):
www.bangor.ac.uk/mindfulness/

Department of Health (DoH):
www.dh.gov.uk

DoH: *Choosing Talking Therapies* booklet:
www.dh.gov.uk/en/Publicationsandstatistics/Publications/
PublicationsPolicyAndGuidance/DH–4008162

Mind (a mental health charity):
www.mind.org.uk

National Institute for Health and Clinical Excellence:
www.nice.org.uk

Pub-Med (free access to some scientific articles):
www.ncbi.nlm.nih.gov/entrez/query.fcgi

Rethink (a mental health charity):
www.rethink.org

The Royal College of Psychiatrists (RCP):
www.rcpsych.ac.uk

RCP antidepressants information:
www.rcpsych.ac.uk/mentalhealthinformation/mental
healthproblems/depression/antidepressants.aspx

Media features

Harris Goldberg, *Numb* [DVD]. US: IMDb; 2007

Victoria Derbyshire BBC2 programme:
http://www.bbc.co.uk/programmes/p05h8drf
https://www.youtube.com/watch?v=GcTXRKVbc00

Jeremy Vine Radio 2 programme:
https://instaud.io/1ug4

British Medical Journal Podcast:
https://m.soundcloud.com/bmjpodcasts/watching-
the-world-through-a-clear-fog-recognising-depersonal
isation-and-derealisation?utm_source=soundcloud&utm_
campaign=share&utm_medium=twitter

Guardian article:
http://www.theguardian.com/society/2015/sep/04/de
personalisation-disorder-the-condition-youve-never-
heard-of-that-affects-millions

Organisations

UK

British Association for Behavioural and Cognitive Psychotherapies (BABCP)
Imperial House, Hornby Street, Bury BL9 5BN
Tel: 0161 705 4304
Email: babcp@babcp.com
Website: www.babcp.com

The British Psychological Society
St Andrews House
48 Princess Road East, Leicester, LE1 7DR
Tel: 0116 254 9568
Email: enquiries@bps.org.uk
Website: www.bps.org.uk

Australia

Mental Health Foundation of Australia
270 Church Street, Richmond, Victoria 3121, Australia
Tel: 03 9427 0406
Email: admin@mentalhealthvic.org.au
Website: www.mentalhealthvic.org.au

USA

Mental Health America
2000 North Beauregard Street, 6th Floor
Alexandria, VA 22311
USA
Tel: (703) 684 7722
Toll-free: (800) 969 6642
Website: www.nmha.org

NARSAD: The Mental Health Research Association
60 Cutter Mill Road,
Suite 404,
Great Neck, NY 11021
USA
Tel: (800) 829 8289
Email: info@narsad.org
Website: www.narsad.org

National Alliance on Mental Illness
3803 N. Fairfax Drive,
Suite 100,
Arlington, VA 22201-3042
USA
Tel: (703) 524 7600
Information helpline: 1-800-950-NAMI (6264)
Website: www.nami.org

National Institute of Mental Health
Public Information and Communications Branch
6001 Executive Boulevard,
Room 8184, MSC 9663,
Bethesda, MD 20892-9663
USA
Tel: (301) 443 4513
Toll-free: 1-866-615-6464
Email: nimhinfo@nih.gov
Website: www.nimh.nih.gov

**National Mental Health Consumers' Self-Help
Clearinghouse**
1211 Chestnut Street,
Suite 1207,
Philadelphia, PA 19107
USA
Tel: (212) 751 1810
Email: info@mhselfhelp.org
Website: www.mhselfhelp.org

Index

NB: page numbers in italic indicate figures or tables